Talking and Doing Science
in the Early Years

Young children are intuitive, emergent scientists – they observe, raise hypotheses, experiment and notice patterns. Most of our everyday actions at home and in other settings, inside and outside, have a scientific basis and it is through these early experiences that children formulate their ideas about the world in which we live.

This accessible book introduces the simplest forms of the principles and big ideas of science and provides a starting point for encouraging children to have an interest and experiential understanding of basic science and engineering. It shows how you can support young children in exploring everyday phenomena and develop their scientific language skills through readily available resources and hands-on experiences. Each chapter focuses on a different aspect of science and includes:

- a summary of the 'big ideas' to refresh your own scientific knowledge;
- numerous activities that encourage young children to observe, question and carry out their own investigations;
- a useful list of everyday resources and relevant vocabulary.

Providing a wealth of exciting, meaningful ways to promote scientific experiences and learning, this highly practical book will help you to build on children's natural curiosity about the world and develop their understanding through your everyday provision in early years settings and at home.

Sue Dale Tunnicliffe is a senior lecturer in Science Education at the Institute of Education, University of London, UK.

Talking and Doing Science in the Early Years

A practical guide for ages 2–7

Sue Dale Tunnicliffe

Routledge
Taylor & Francis Group

LONDON AND NEW YORK

First published 2013
by Routledge
2 Park Square, Milton Park, Abingdon, Oxon OX14 4RN

Simultaneously published in the USA and Canada
by Routledge
711 Third Avenue, New York, NY 10017

Routledge is an imprint of the Taylor & Francis Group, an informa business

British Library Cataloguing in Publication Data
A catalogue record for this book is available from the British Library

Library of Congress Cataloging in Publication Data
Tunnicliffe, Sue Dale.
  Talking and doing science in the early years : a practical guide for ages
  2–7/Sue Dale Tunnicliffe.—First edition.
    pages cm
  Includes bibliographical references.
  1. Science—Study and teaching (Early childhood)—United States.
  I. Title.
  LB1139.5.S35T86 2013
  372.35—dc23

                                                    2012039579

ISBN: 978–0–415–69089–8 (hbk)
ISBN: 978–0–415–69090–4 (pbk)
ISBN: 978–0–203–16380–1 (ebk)

Typeset in Optima
by RefineCatch Limited, Bungay, Suffolk

MIX
Paper from
responsible sources
FSC   FSC® C013056
www.fsc.org

Printed and bound in Great Britain by
TJ International Ltd, Padstow, Cornwall

In memory of my eldest son
Alan Dale Tunnicliffe
29.9.1971 to 18.1.2009
Who showed me how young children find out about science

Contents

Figures

Acknowledgements

I thank first of all my late eldest son, Alan, who was so intrigued as a small child by the world around him that he showed me the essence of learning science that changed my whole perspective. He showed me the vital role that early encounters with the everyday world contribute to science education; a tradition carried on by my grandsons. I learned that I needed to observe the children and listen to them, not to tell all that I knew, and that I only needed to give them vocabulary and explain simply in their terms. I had to think hard about what really were the fundamental ideas in the everyday science we explored, and not to give simplified versions of the conventional explanation I'd been told and learnt at school and university. I apologize to those pupils from my early days of teaching in grammar schools and primary schools, whom I probably lectured without listening to them and their understandings very much!

I acknowledge the assistance, advice and other contributions and comments made to me during the writing of this book by former students: Nigel Edwards, Táahira Said-Beg, Iteen Palmer and Naseen Salami in particular.

Finally, I thank my husband for always putting up with bits and pieces around the house that I said were essential for my science teaching and learning!

Sue Dale Tunnicliffe
Bracknell, Berkshire
2013

About the book

Summary

The function of this book in encouraging talking while doing science activities in the early years is discussed, and a theoretical perspective of the importance of the development of language and observation is put forward. The emergence of the child as an intuitive scientist is first stated, and the role of the adult as essential facilitator is described. The purpose of the book and structure is explained. Learning science in the early years is a collaboration between adult and child.

Introduction

Just as there is a critical period for language acquisition in the early years, I believe that there is one for the development of an understanding of science phenomena. The first observations and hands-on experiences of children in the everyday world, which are science in action, are crucial for their future learning. The role of the adult in facilitating such opportunities and talking with the children is key, forming the most important part of a child's education, although these early years are not considered those of formal schooling.

This book provides some experiences and investigations for these early science learners (who spontaneously have an investigative and inquisitive approach to the world around them) that can be carried out in the home, nurseries and playgroups as well as outdoors in playgrounds, parks, gardens or when walking in the streets. These investigations are not examples of formal science teaching. We are not setting out to teach the children science. Rather, we are seeking to provide them with experiences and language so that once the children are being taught they might understand the theory, having had relevant experiences. Tracing backwards from the advanced concepts of school and even later science learning, it is easy to identify the very first or fundamental ideas on which this later theory is based. These ideas or concepts are what this book sets out through various experiences for the children. Often, people qualified in science know too much and find it difficult to undo this later learning to focus on the basic ideas.

Expensive equipment is not needed to provide hands-on experiences in science in these essential early interactions. Items that are available in an ordinary home or setting provide the necessary equipment, as do the everyday varied environments that a child encounters.

The adults do not need to be formal science educators. All adults working with young children are science educators because they are aware of the experiences and observations that there are for the developing child to encounter. Talking about these, with the child asking questions, wondering what and why, is a vital element in the development of understanding, communication and social skills. Without these early first encounters the child misses crucial experiences. They are the most important in the child's science learning.

About this book

This book is designed to provide educators who interact with young children aged seven and under with starting points to help them develop play and talk with the children in their care. It is not about teaching the theory of science but about noticing and experiencing everyday science in action. Science is based on observations that give rise to learning language, formulating questions and further investigations, as well as developing communication and social skills. However, many parents, carers and early years educators feel that they don't know enough science to be able to effectively introduce their charges to this area of learning.

This book introduces any educator of preschool children to the simplest form of the principles and big ideas of science (Harlen, 2010). It is an essential start to encouraging children to have an interest and experiential understanding, at a basic level, of science and engineering and links the foundation upon which formal school studies are built.

Organization of the book

The first three chapters, including this one, set the scene for *Talking and Doing Science*. Information is provided about language, with some vocabulary suggestions as well as prompts for asking questions and developing dialogue with these young learners. Chapter 2 focuses on language and everyday science, talking with children and their intuitive behaviours as emergent scientists. Chapter 3 has some suggestions for resources that are useful in the learning setting and readily available, at low cost.

The areas of science that each chapter deals with are indicated below:

- Biological Science

  Chapter 4: Ourselves

  Chapter 5: Other animals

  Chapter 6: Plants

  Chapter 7: Other living things

- Physical Science

  Chapter 8: Forces

  Chapter 9: Structures

  Chapter 10: Changes

  Chapter 11: Materials

- Environmental Science

  Chapter 12: Built environment

  Chapter 13: Outside

Each chapter begins with a summary and the key words associated with the topic, so that you can look them up for further clarity should you wish to. A section on 'Big Ideas' follows. These sections are designed to refresh your memory about the scientific background to the topic on which the activities for the children are focused. They are not intended for you to tell to the children.

These early learners need the hands-on experience together with the relevant everyday words and dialogue about the topic, but not the theory. Other people can develop that later. Following these first sections, each chapter contains a series of 'Talking and Doing' activities that can be presented to children, starting with the simplest. The resources required are those readily available, from everyday locations. Refer to the equipment list in Chapter 2 for ideas, if you need any.

Activities may be whole group, a small number of children or one-to-one, depending on the number of children, the organization of the area and the situation.

In the activities section, 'Talking and Doing', the initial activities are for the youngest children, so they can hear the relevant words associated with what they refer to. Key words are provided in vocabulary lists. Select words from here if you want further ideas to follow on from those you already have. Without this language relationship to objects and actions, the children are hampered from making further progress. Talking to them is the most important start in science and engineering learning.

It is hoped that the adults working with the children will integrate the activities with others, such as drawing, painting, modelling, story reading and telling, drama recording and communicating, so that the science is part of a holistic experience. I hope that this book will help you, the reader, to support your children's scientific learning, with enjoyment for all of you.

2 | Background to early years science

Emphasis of early years science

There has been a paradigm shift from focusing on secondary pupils to encourage them to study science to a realization that a sound basis from the earliest years is the most effective route to educating children in science. Research (e.g. Lyons Report, Tytler Report from Australia) shows that children in their early teens have already made up their minds about science, and the work of Tymms and Harlen (2009) in England suggests children have formed their attitudes towards science by the age of nine. Most often they are not enthused by the subject encountered in school. Alison Gopnik's (2009) book shows, from extensive research, that children are intuitive scientists in their early years before formal schooling; they observe, raise hypotheses, experiment and notice patterns, the basis for statistics and evidence.

Development of the child as a scientist

During their early years, children acquire an understanding of occurrences, behaviours and objects and acquire basic science skills of observing, questioning and investigating, known as process skills (Eshach & Fried, 2005). These fundamental skills begin in infancy as the new being starts developing, and prowess in these skills and processes increases as the child ages (Lind, 1999; Piaget & Inhelder, 2000). In these early years, children develop a feel- and experiential-based understanding of everyday science and engineering phenomena, and such these years are deemed of great importance by researchers, e.g. Eshach and Fried (2005). However, it has been found (Sackes et al., 2011) that science experiences in formal early years education are not reliable fore-casters of future achievement in formal science learning in later schooling. Furthermore, the attitude of preschool teachers towards science influences children. If the teacher displays wonder and excitement, children think science and its associated subjects are exciting too (Spektor-Levy et al., 2011). Presumably the same effect is noticed in the behaviours of any adult with whom these early learners are in contact. It is thus important to remember that it is not the content knowledge of the adult that is important, but the curiosity and enthusiasm that s/he shows.

Talk with doing

Young children need first-hand, concrete learning experiences with appropriate talk. They need to hear the words of science and engineering in the everyday even before they can talk, as during this period they can still see and hear. Sadly, in today's world there seems to be little time for quality talk in some homes, and less and less time at school. In recent years the importance of 'talk for learning' has been recognized, but we tend to move too quickly into talk relating to abstract learning.

There is an increasing recognition of the importance of the early years of a child and the interventions that are so crucial for children's healthy development. The years 0–7 are those most important in a child's learning and the opportunities and experiences in these early years lay the firm foundations for later learning. Such opportunities, if not spontaneously and intuitively provided, need to be planned and provided through early intervention strategies as recommended by some governments:

> The first few years of a child's life are fundamentally important. Evidence tells us that they shape children's future development, and influence how well children do at school, their ongoing health and wellbeing and their achievements later in life. The Government is clear that all young children, whatever their background or current circumstances, deserve the best possible start in life and must be given the opportunity to fulfil their potential.
>
> (Dfe, 2011)

Surely, talking and doing everyday science and engineering during a child's early years is part of this aspiration for all children?

Scientific literacy for all

In many countries of the world, including the UK, it is a goal to promote scientific literacy for citizens, although among under-represented groups, science learning divorced from everyday life alienates many children. Primary science in schools has, since it was introduced in England in the national curriculum in 1988, striven to make the things learned relevant to everyday (Scribner-MacLean, 1996), but it still misses the fundamental concept of focus on early years science before the onset of formal schooling.

The language development through science work

Observation and experience are the foundation of science learning, together with informing the child of names of things and processes; but this early stage has to be experiential and in partnership with a facilitator who can provide the labels for the phenomenon and activities observed, such as pouring and pushing.

Young children ask questions incessantly when given an opportunity (Tough, 1977), a behaviour that often disappears in the formal education environment where classic triadic dialogue takes over. However, there is a move towards developing dialogic talking in classrooms (Alexander, 2008), and argumentation. Yet young children can be inducted into such an approach before school tuition begins; indeed, many carers of preschool children carry out this type of dialogue, asking 'Why?' to a child: 'Why do you do that?' 'What did you see?'

Children need to develop the language needed to enable them to ask questions and justify their ideas as intuitive scientists (Gopnik, 2009). Learning language in a meaningful context, exploring the everyday world, is an optimum means of developing both language skills and prowess as well as learning fundamental science. Children should be encouraged to relate what they notice and observe to what they already know, interpreting and making sense of objects and other phenomena for themselves. Take this example: A four-year-old examining things on a discovery table in her preschool picked up some seashells and looked at them. One was spiral in shape; she looked, then smiled and shouted, 'Here is an ice-cream cone!' She was associating the shape of the shell with the ice-cream cone with which she was familiar.

Talking and listening

Constructing meaning about the world is a social activity (Bruner, 1990) and meaning is heard through voices. Thus, analysis of conversations is a good idea, developing further from just assessing the initial form and function of talk used with different ages of children. Conversations can be categorized according to complexity of structure and content, known as 'Labeling conversation'. There is a notable progression in the types of conversations recognized: First of all, heard with babies/toddlers, is telling the child a name for something, even before the child talks. Then adults often open with a question drawing attention to the specimen, before giving it a name that the child repeats once s/he talks, as children that age often delight in doing. The adult, often the mother, closes these conversations with praise; an example of classic IRE, initiation–response–evaluation dialogue (Chin, 2007), which can then be followed up by further talk and activities. Often adults talk with preschool children who have developed further than just naming or labeling using 'baby words'; for example, 'Mum, look! A birdie!' Conversation initiated by the child is called inverse triadic dialogue, where the child starts and closes the conversation (Patrick & Tunnicliffe, 2012), followed by dialogic talk (Alexander, 2008), the basis for science investigations.

Learning science is talking science, not teaching and telling. Talking and listening are two of the four strands of literacy, and the first stages in literacy are acquired if children are living in an environment where they hear language. Language is a means for thinking collectively (Mercer, 2000), which is what occurs between an adult and child when the child wants to show something or the adult wants to recognize the interest a child is showing about something. Mothers and carers usually spontaneously name things and point phenomena out to children in their earliest years from the time they are born.

The starting point for science is observation, and adults working with early years children can share and talk about observations, thus possibly increasing their own self-esteem and confidence about scientific phenomena because they often realize that they can recognize and talk about everyday science and engineering.

> Children, we now know, need to talk, and to experience a rich diet of spoken language in order to think and learn. Reading, writing and number may be acknowledged as curriculum basics but talk is the true foundation for teaching.
>
> (Alexander, 2008: 9)

The ideas of children

Through their observations and investigations, as well as applying their logic, children develop ideas about particular causes of phenomena. Such ideas are often different to those of accepted science. These explanations or ideas are often referred to as misconceptions or alternative conceptions. They are very real to the children and are often difficult for adults to change when the child is older; thus, these early ideas can form barriers to further learning and understanding. For example, a four-year-old child had his own explanation about why it rains and announced, 'It rains because the sun shines on the tops of the clouds and pushes the rain out and it rains down to us' (Bradley, 1996: 3). It is also apparent that the taxonomy of animals used spontaneously by young children is not taxonomy at one with that of biology.

Science of everyday

Learning science is looking at phenomena, everyday and unusual, but looking with meaning, in other words, observing. Such looking and noticing happens before children talk, for they are listening to what their adults and others say about the objects and happenings. Once they talk they are naming what they see and asking about these things comes naturally and spontaneously to most young children. Preschool children are by nature scientists and they notice patterns. The same action they make or see repeatedly results in the same outcome every time, such as dropping an object from a height such as from a pushchair or high chair. The fact that this is accepted as physics phenomena and is the effect principally of gravity and mass of the dropped object depending on the object dropping does not matter to the child in this beginning science stage. Such observations are at the start of experimental evidence and data collection, and thus statistics. The young scientist is establishing an understanding of apparatus. However, an adult alert to opportunities to develop the observations and experiences of the child through talking to him or her can help children even more in their learning of science.

Cooking changes ingredients. Consider eggs cooking. If a child looks at the raw egg first, s/he will notice that when the inside of the egg is released from its enclosing shell it is not the same shape as the egg. Then the yellow albumen (the thick liquid around the yoke) is talked about and as the egg cooks the adult draws attention to what happens. Gradually the yellow fluid changes to a solid white material as the egg cooks. Such observations are the basis of chemistry, for this is a chemical reaction.

Investigations

Observation is the key to beginning science and looking and noticing is the key. Young children have the time to stand, stare, ponder and make their own observations in this way. They are experiencing and learning the manifestation of the basics of science even if they can not yet speak in order to question. Before a child talks, his or her adult often poses questions such as 'I wonder what would happen if we . . .?' The children become used to hearing this pattern of talking, which is key to scientific learning and experimental investigations. 'I wonder what . . .' is the beginning of hypothesis making. 'I think so and so will happen' is the start of formulating and making a prediction. Actually doing whatever was suggested is the beginning of experimental investigations.

Such an activity also involves a key aspect of learning science, that of logistics. In order to do many investigations you require the appropriate resources (fulfilling the role that specialized equipment plays in laboratories and field work) to carry out your plan. However, science learning is not about being given items to use in an investigation; it is about deciding what the individual wants to do in his or her investigations. Of course there has to be an element of instruction with some items, such as learning the skill of measuring and pouring an amount of water, weighing an object or amount using scales, but such skills are often learnt as part of being at home, in play at preschool or in child care.

Young children that achieve something are usually so excited that they tell everyone and even before being able to speak will lead their adult to see what it is they have observed, found or done. Adults with young children can support such a pattern of activities, saying the words appropriate to the actions and names of an object. Hearing appropriate language for things and actions is a vital part of foundation learning in science and engineering.

Language acquisition

The first stage in language acquisition is learning the name of things: live organisms; natural phenomena such as weather, stones and water; constructed objects such as buildings, jugs and bags; and actions such as walking, pouring, holding and pushing. This is the 'labelling' stage of learning language (Bruner, 1990). First, educators name things and actions in their everyday environment for their children and subsequently often refer to the item in a 'Motherese' term, baby talk that children also invent for themselves as they learn to talk.

A young boy of my acquaintance, upon being told a large vehicle down the road was a digger, referred to it, and any other vehicle for a while, as a 'dig-dig'. Adults will frequently use 'baby words'; for instance, I heard the mother of a toddler in a zoo refer to a vulture in an enclosure as a 'birdie'. One of my grandsons, when on the river (in a boat for the first time), was very excited by all the ducks and was resistant to being told that the big white 'ducks' were called swans, the small black birds with a white patch on their head were coots and the large grey 'ducks' were geese. He was still at the stage when all birds belonged to the category of 'duck' and had not yet acquired the concept that ducks were a particular type of bird. Mariyah, at 20 months old, saw a plane in the sky and called it a 'bird' because it was flying, and while watching a wildlife programme on the television she called a frog 'fish' because it was swimming in the water. She also said 'up' as she was with her family driving up a hill, but as the car then went down the other side, she said 'Wheee' instead of 'down'. We think she associated the 'down action' with coming down a slide or stairs because her parents have said that to her when on a slide or coming down some steps.

A child's first word

It is an interesting exercise to write down on a significant date in the child's life the words that s/he says. Here is the list of words that my eldest son could say with understanding on his second birthday.

Alan's words on his second birthday 29.9.73

Baby	That	Egg	Balloon
Church	Hello	Iron	Goat
Eye	Scissors	Onion	Pineapple
Hair	Down	Alan	School
Two	Orange	Dig-dig	Plane
Hand	Dog	Bee	Big
Shoe	Hen	Hole	Sauce
Shell	Fridge	Man	Teeth
Horse	Ball	Stool	Chin
Cat	Gate	Bit	Circle
Daddy	Biscuit	Towel	Lawn
Post	Ear	Drawer	Shoulder
Bricks	Kate	Girl	Mouth
Dougal (his toy dog)	Spade	Another	Nose
Bye	There	Broken	Peter
Coat	Bridge	Turn	Clock
Bang	Me	Machine	Phone
Barrow	Bike	I	Shave
Dig	Shut	Am	Mend
Out	Tea	Clap	
Spoon	Splash	Tick	
Toast	Brush	Milk	
Toes	Push	Ring	
Boots	Door	Peep	
Beans	Home	Mine	
Bus	House	Bed	
Date	Here	Comb	
This	Boat	Are	
		Plate	

The adults with whom children explore the environment, inside or out, have a tremendously important role in influencing what the children observe.

> The experiences which children have of adults using language with them must play an important part in influencing the kind of interpretation that children will make of their everyday experiences.… If for example, the adult is talking about particular detail in the environment, the structure of plants, the shape and colour of the rainbow, the reflections in puddles, then the child's attention is being drawn to objects that he might not have noticed had no one spoken to him about them, or, if he had, might have remained at a level of interpretation that did not require conscious awareness of detail.
>
> (Tough, 1977: 35)

Vygotsky, the Russian psychologist (1962, 1978), pointed out the importance of language and social interaction in learning. Language has two roles: first in social interactions between people where it acts as a social tool; and second used in our midst for organizing an individual's thinking. Hence, it can be regarded as a psychological tool.

Helping children talk to clarify ideas

Signaling and then talking about their observations and ideas helps children clarify their observations and thoughts about them. People use language as a tool for thinking and are helped in this thinking by others using the same language. Mercer et al. (2004) coined the term 'exploratory' talk for when children hold critical, yet constructive conversations with each other. Indeed, there is the view (e.g. Rogoff, 1990) that the growing-up of humans is an apprenticeship in thinking, and is learnt through dialogues both heard and in which each apprentice participates, defined by the culture in which the child exists.

Using talk to focus a child's attention

The language used by adults to a child focuses his or her attention on aspects of the immediate environment and thus the presence of an adult affects the conversational behaviour. Furthermore, if the child has brought a phenomenon to the attention of the adult, or the adult notices the interest shown by the child, the language and social interaction used are important in the consolidation of learning. The adult's ability to easily converse with the child is key; in later science learning, the capability of reasoning is essential in the constructing valid scientific arguments, and young children learn this from their adult (Wellington & Osborne, 2010). Early years children can listen to an adult reasoning about whatever the focus of interest is and hear the 'way it is done', using evidence and knowledge in constructing a rational dialogue.

Children need to be asked why they think such and such; What have they seen? Have they seen something like that before? Where? What did they think?

Saidja's bumble bee

A four-year-old girl rushed into the Early Learning Room, so excited because she had found a dead bumble bee. It was, she said, 'a Mummy Bee!' On being asked how she knew it was a mummy bee she shrugged and said it must be a mummy because you get lots of bumble bees. She was not asked why she thought it was a bee; no questions about what features she recognized that made it a member of the category bumble bees, or if it was an insect, or any biological queries of a similar nature. Saidja was however so motivated that she went and wrote that she had found a bumble bee on a piece of paper. She had something to write about and she wished to do so. This was writing with meaning.

Adults using talk to help learning

Adults trying to help children learn use talk to elicit relevant knowledge from the learner, to respond to things that they say and describe the experiences they share with the children in a meaningful way (Mercer, 2000). Educators develop their dialogue to tell a story, which is frequently that of a scientific explanation for a phenomenon. These adults set the scene and create a need for an explanation (outcome of the story), which they do through eliciting differences of opinions from learners: promising clarification, using other stories to suggest ideas creating expectations, showing counterintuitive results. Adults with very young children comment upon what is seen and link their words to what they know the child has noticed before, thus basing the new dialogue on the child's repertoire of experience.

Story telling

Adults insert a variety of methods of adult–early learner verbal interactions into their story telling, which provide further meaning. These include demonstrations, practical investigations, discussion and explanations. Distinct types of explanation used are knowledge and ideas of children; explaining in a story; delivering a new vision of how things are and practising using relevant language. Explanations depend on the knowledge, experience and resources of the person working with the early learners, the nature of the subject matter and the manner in which the work develops. This is the same procedure as that carried out by teachers later on with older children in school. While these ways of talking have been studied in the classroom, they are equally applicable to the home and other settings. Furthermore, different techniques for telling a story are likely to form part of the way in which parents help provide further meaning about what is observed for their children.

Conclusion

The message of this book is that talking and doing go hand in hand as children explore their everyday world with a supportive adult.

3 | Resources, language and skills for everyday science

Summary

This chapter is concerned with Big Ideas about language and science learning. The planning of science-based activities is discussed with regards to the vocabulary that could be used and ways of initiating a dialogue with the learner through questions. A vocabulary list is included for reference. The use of everyday basic items and simple equipment is discussed along with a suggested equipment list. Special issues concerning bilingual children and the importance of play are put forward. The role of the adult in supporting the child and recognizing science opportunities and activities, and the encouragement of further achievement by children are considered.

Introduction

Sometimes the opportunity for a science activity will arise through a child's questions or observations. A key skill of early years workers is to recognize such openings and develop the learning opportunity there and then. Such spontaneous occurrences are a hallmark of young children coming from other activities or observations. At other times you will have decided, as a sole facilitator or as part of a team, that on that day you are going to organize activities and make opportunities for observation and exploration, such as water play, a shape hunt or a walk to look at the plants around. Spontaneous activities can be organized and developed there and then but they still will follow a fixed pattern, explored in this chapter.

The following sections are for guidance when organizing your activities.

Investigating: before embarking on the activity

When planning what to do, bear in mind the following organizational aspects:

- available space for talking, thinking and doing;
- equipment/ resource availability and location;
- adult help;
- other activities in the room;
- needs of children;
- vocabulary to be used;
- questions to use;
- the pre-experiences that the child needs before s/he can effectively be involved in this one, such as knowing water is wet and that it takes the shape of its container in the case of washing up.

Children learn by doing. Their initial discussion is a form of predicting and their predictions will be a refinement of what they think will happen based on previous experiences (hypotheses). Their ideas may be to us extravagant, but with practice and hands-on experience the children refine their ideas and expectations.

Points to consider

When planning any experiences, bear in mind:

- The aims of the activities. There are often two aims in everyday tasks that provide starting science activities: those of the science and those of everyday life. For example, washing up for you, but learning about the properties of water and soap and the actions of a force with a cloth on a plate with dirt on it for the child.
- Details of appropriate pre-experience (if the children do not have the pre-experience suggested it is important to allow some time for free play with the equipment).

Equipment

All the activities in the book use familiar everyday items or those readily found in playgroups and reception classes. Many can be bought from suppliers of early years educational materials.

The following is a list of some basic items with which science can be experienced in the early years:

- *Kitchen equipment and containers*: Plastic dishes and trays, yoghurt pots or similar plastic containers, plastic beakers, card beakers, mugs, dishes, wooden spoons, metal spoons, plastic spoons, serving spoons, forks, knives, stirrers, bowls of various sizes, jugs of various sizes, measuring jugs, syringes (such as the ones uses for giving liquid measures), plastic lids and bottle tops, scales, paper straws, plastic straws, bendy straws, kitchen towels and filter papers, cooking ingredients, vinegar, bicarbonate of soda, salt, sugar, soda of some type in a screw top bottle, washing up liquid, soap, ice trays and fridge, stove or heat source.

- *Household equipment*: Mirrors, fridge magnets, torches and other items of the household with batteries, string, play dough, paper, cardboard, card pieces, construction paper, wax paper, various pieces of fabric, pencils, wax crayons, felt tip pens, pieces of chalk, hole punchers, sellotape, rubber bands, balloons, toy cars, building blocks, tapes, zip lock bags, cardboard tubes, magnifying glasses, cameras, wipes, plastic covers for tables, flip-flops, trainers, slippers, empty boxes of various sizes, droppers.

- *Pictures*: Pictures, posters and clippings from journals and newspapers of animals, plants and natural phenomena such as wetlands, streams, ponds, seas, rivers, volcanoes, rock formations.

- *Outdoor equipment*: Heat strips, potted plants, plant pots, seed trays, seeds, soil, trowels, plant cuttings, plantlets (e.g. spider plants), willow twigs, piece of soft wood cut across, pebbles, stones, fossils, play sand, marble chippings, small watering can, wellington boots, rain hats, umbrellas, plastic sheeting.

Ideas for discussion questions before and after activities

The discussion questions before and after the activities are solely suggestions to initiate the dialogue with the children and are provided for those adult workers who find it a little difficult to get started in the discussion. Often just using one of the questions suggested triggers dialogue and no more of the set questions are needed.

A list of related vocabulary for the adult

For the suggested activities in this book there is a suggested vocabulary list in a later section. This is provided as a trigger for the adult who may wish to plan the use of these key words for each activity into his/her dialogue. If they are not appropriate words to use with a particular set of children or need extending further the adult will make this decision.

Information giving is the keystone of teaching and learning. Once a child has words to use, listening to his or her explanations and decisions about objects and actions is vital for his or her scientific development. Helping a child to find out more through questioning is crucial in developing everyday and later science. Effective questioning is central to science learning and an essential component of talking science.

Vocabulary and questions

Talking science obviously involves language, and talking is an important part of problem solving. This may be a process you wish to introduce to the children with whom you are working, challenging these early learners to find an answer through observations or experimentation in relation to a challenge you set (Tunnicliffe, 1990); alternatively, you could encourage them to think about before and after situations and then 'Think and Do' (Tunnicliffe, 1989). Children should be encouraged to talk about topics that engage their interest, what they see and about anything that they remember about this situation or phenomena that they have met previously.

While these early learners may hear many everyday words that are sufficient for what you need to talk about, there is mathematical and scientific terminology that can be introduced into your conversations, as well as everyday English terms for different actions, positions, resources, movements and materials.

Questioning

Once observations are made, which is very much what talking science is, children begin to question and ask, 'Why?' In many instances of physical science, you can ask 'What happens if . . .?' and suggest that the children could perform some action or investigation to find out, suggesting indeed what might happen. This is the beginning of putting forward a hypothesis, part of the science process and as children gather more concrete experiences of their everyday world, they begin to use what they have already learnt and observed in forming their ideas of what they want to do to test out their theories. They use rapaciously acquired skills and knowledge. In formal education these stages become slotted into levels and when a child has acquired competency in an action or thought s/he are said to have attained that level of development. In biological observations they often make longer observations by first looking and often touching or otherwise observing and then asking questions, which would lead to more advanced science investigations to formulate experiments to find the answer. For example, when looking at some fish in a stream, a three-year-old wanted to know what they were (a labeling activity, learning the name), and then what they ate. He made a few suggestions such as the weed he could see, but those thoughts went no further.

Looking then investigating: a child's approach

Another early years child wanted to know about the petals on a flower in the garden.

First he looked hard and long, then he touched a petal, next he pulled its tip (applying a force!) and observed what happened. He had pulled off the petal. Petals were removable! He had conducted an investigation of his own without formally announcing his thoughts and the science process; he did a spontaneous investigation. He did not talk aloud but obviously was thinking to himself.

Starting the questioning or observational dialogue

Starting a dialogue can sometimes be difficult, so it is useful to have some techniques to use to help. The following section introduces the beginnings of questions, called 'stems', as well as vocabulary in different categories, which may be useful in thinking of your dialogue. You could perhaps make a list of these words and others that you consider relevant to tasks and talk you and the children are undertaking and keep a record of which are used and which a child enjoys and feels more comfortable using.

Stems are the words used at the beginning of a sentence, particularly in the case of a question but also in directed observations. Often used stems in science talk are as follows:

- Can you . . .? E.g. Can you see that cloud in the sky? Can you hear that noise?
- What is . . .? E.g. What colour is that plant?
- Where is . . .? E.g. Where is that noise coming from?
- How can we be sure that is . . .? E.g. How can we be sure that is water?
- What is the same and what is different about . . .? E.g. Two clay shapes of similar size but different colours.
- Why do ____, ____ and ____ look similar? E.g. Of the two green plants one has flowers, the other does not, one has leaves with parallel venation, one has leaves with branched venation.
- What is different about . . .? E.g. The two green plants.
- How would you explain . . .? E.g. Two flowers on stems each in a vase, one vase has no water and the flower stem has drooped.
- Where do you think that . . .? E.g. Animal lives; after seeing a bumble bee in a garden on a flower.
- Why do you think . . .? E.g. Why do you think the bumble bee lives on the plant?
- What does that animal tell us about itself and what it eats? E.g. Watching a butterfly or bee in a flower gathering pollen.
- What is shared by . . .? E.g. Two different shapes that weigh the same amount.
- Why is . . .? E.g. The puddle disappearing, the sun 'gone in'?

- Is there . . .? E.g. The same amount of water in this beaker as there was in the jug before you poured all the water out of the jug into the beaker?
- How did . . .? E.g. How did you change the shape of that piece of clay?

Bilingual children

Some children speak one language at home and another in school. Twenty-five per cent of Welsh schools are Welsh medium but some of these children are reading and talking at home in English, so they are bilingual. Other children come to a country from another with a very different culture and mother tongue, which is not available in their new school. These children require special awareness. Statistics taken from the school censure, as featured in the *Guardian* newspaper on 22nd June 2011, show that 24.3 per cent of all pupils in English state schools (primary and secondary) were from an ethnic minority, an increase from 19.8 per cent five years before (Shepherd, 2011).

The number of children in English secondary schools whose first language was not English was 12.3 per cent, a rise from 10.5 per cent in 2006. Two London boroughs, Newham and Tower Hamlets, had 78 per cent and 74 per cent respectively of primary school children whose first language was not English (Shepherd, 2011). Such children have particular needs; a small study in 2011 investigated the understanding and knowledge of everyday plants and animals among bilingual children in a North London preschool. The results showed that that pupils referenced the home as the source of their learning and not school. They recognized animals and plants with which they came into contact, named their habitats, used scientific naming that improved their English language and recognized the contributions of both their home, culture and first language to their learning (Palmer, in press).

Children's technique of identifying objects

Children match what they know to what they see and identify accordingly. A toddler watching penguins at a zoo floating on the water, waiting for the keeper to bring their fish at feeding time, said to his mother that they were ducks. Floating penguins do indeed resemble ducks; only when they clambered out for the fish the keeper bought to the side could the child see that they were not ducks.

Skills for everyday science

Children need to be able to sense their everyday environment by seeing, hearing and touching as well as feeling the environment through ambient temperature or wind presence and speed. If children are physically capable of doing so they need the manipulative skills of holding, picking items up and putting them down, of touching and feeling gently, of being aware of smells and other feelings that abound in our everyday environments.

Starting the science process

Science is not only about content, information and facts; it is about the process of doing science. This starts with an observation, noticing, asking what something is, learning objects or happenings, naming or labeling and noticing features and properties about whatever the object is; its colour, shape, sound. These young investigators (Gopnik, 2009) spontaneously observe things and ask questions, think of investigations, try things out, see patterns (collecting data) and often draw conclusions, frequently sharing what they have found out from their investigations.

A baby's first investigation exemplar

Babies in a highchair, pram or pushchair usually drop an object over the side, again and again and again, providing someone else picks up the object and gives it back to them, and they repeat the experiment. This is a scientific investigation; each time the item is let go it drops to the ground.

Science educators try to formalize the science process. It is often easier to see this process in physical activities rather than biology, which is concerned with organisms and what they look like, where they live and their habitat and wider environment.

Babies thus learn about the world around them in the same way older people learn science for themselves as individuals or researchers. The characteristic of science is experimenting and analyzing the data obtained as well as composing explanations or theories about the world, physical, biological and emotional. One of the problems for adults trying to understand how the very young learn science is that babies don't talk a lot, or at all, in their earliest years. Therefore, psychologists have studied what babies do, interpreted their actions and decided they are working in the scientific method. Parents and people working with the youngest children notice that babies are intrigued by new objects and actions and can work out the feelings of adults in certain instances (Gopnik & Seiver, 2009) and alter their actions so as to please or help the adult.

Instinctive physics

Researchers have found that babies in fact have a perhaps instinctive feel for physics, such as the path along which an object moves and gravity, as exemplified by the highchair. Babies are intrigued when they observe an event that does not fit in with their understanding of what should happen. Young children can work out cause and effect too and if given something will investigate to see what happens. They can very quickly work out how to make something simple work, like the mouse of a computer, or a television controller. Moreover, they often experiment until they obtain a result. Play is thus an exploring of their world and objects and other phenomena within it that they encounter.

Actions of young children as part of the scientific method

The following information is to advise you how the activities that you are observing, facilitating or actually sharing with children fit into the theoretical structure of a science investigation. Through encouraging young children to follow their intuitive scientific instinct it really is laying the foundation for further science and language work for life-long learning and a head-start for when they start formal education. It does not mean you have to make home or investigative setting experiences fit their explorations. That may come at school, when we hope they will become firmly established as apprentice scientists.

Equipment for observations

Science is often about observing, and sometimes we use equipment to assist in the process. Describing observations is the first stage in using equipment; perhaps when the children use a magnifying glass or sheet to look at a flower such as a lily, seeing the pollen grains (male sex cells) on the stamens (male sex organs) or to see an ice cube melting. Often scientists measure their investigations in some way; it might be measuring the amount of liquid they have added to something, weighing out the items they have used just as we do with ingredients when cooking, marking the length of the distance something moves or the temperature of something else.

Measurement

Young children often spontaneously and instinctively use non-standard measures: the number of their paces or steps their toy car travelled, for instance; the hotness of some-thing using their hands; the weight of something by picking it up or comparing the weight of two similar things, one in each hand, to decide which is the heaviest. They may measure an amount of a liquid by repeatedly filling a container using another container that they know, such as their drinking beaker, until all the fluid has been emptied. Then, for example, a bottle might contain three beakers-full of the drink. Many young children are familiar with taking medicine, which might be a medical spoonful but more likely these days given as the measure of the liquid in a small syringe. Again this is a measure, although in the case of the syringe it is calibrated and an excel-lent tool for introducing children to standard measures. Other ways of bringing standard measures to their attention is the use of temperature or fever strips for body heat, rulers and tape measures for distance and height, scales and balance for the weights of items such as a suitcase when going on holiday or in cooking where they help weigh out the ingredients using masses of known amounts. If the child can select the appropriate way to measure something and is able to select the appropriate instrument to use, s/he is becoming quite advanced! Once at school s/he will meet the scientific and mathematical apparatus used academically.

Fair tests

The recognition of variables in investigations is an important part of the science process. Traditionally, an early learner of science has to be told what to do, but most children in the everyday world do these actions spontaneously because of their inherent natural curiosity. They are soon able to point out the differences between the start of their investigation and the end, such as in food preparation, the difference between the ingredients at the start when uncooked and the outcome of the meal, the cooked food. They can tell you what has changed. In science terms the things that changed are the dependent variables and the treatment that happened (in this case the cooking at a certain temperature) is the independent variable, with everything else staying the same as control variables.

It's not fair!

Children often say things are not fair and this is recognition that not everything is the same. In primary science work children are expected to be able to design their own investigations as fair tests and identify what changes, what stays the same and the one element of the investigation that is changed.

Recording and communicating actions and findings

Talking science is the beginning of science communication when they talk to you about what they are doing and answer questions. Often children will draw or act out an interesting experience such as flying a kite after they have joined in with this activity, or pretending to be a baby chicken hatching out of an egg after seeing this occur. As they learn further science in formal education, children are expected to be able to record what they do and thus communicate to others their ideas, action plan, results and what they found out.

Observing over time

Children talk about what they notice, and this ability is the start of drawing inferences; the ability to be able to identify and verbalize differences between items, such as a tall tree and a low bush or a red car and a blue car, a white solution and a red one, a heavy ball and a lighter one, is the beginning of this scientific skill. A development of this ability is to be able to recognize that things may change over time. The fact that in winter an apple tree has no leaves and no apples comes as a surprise to young children if they have first seen such a tree in the summer when it had fruit and leaves. When they visit the garden again and rush out to see the apples on the tree, they are perplexed that there are first of all no apples, and second no leaves, leaving a bare tree.

Role of adult

By being with early years children, an adult can ensure that experiences that introduce and develop the skills mentioned above are available and even introduced to them along with the language and forms of talk such as questions. Adults naturally use several techniques when talking to very young children. In the first years of their child's life mothers often make a commentary about what they are doing, what is happening and what actions and objects are involved. Some mothers even label items with name cards and say the name while pointing at the written words. They use two ways of speaking, referred to by Wertsch (1985) as establishing a referential perspective. When the adult realizes the child with whom s/he is talking does not understand, the adult finds something about which the child has understanding. For example, had my grandson never seen a duck or other water bird and showed incomprehension of that subordinate category of bird, I could have talked about the duck being a kind of bird like the one that comes to the bird table in the garden.

When the adult thinks that there is shared knowledge between him and her and the child s/he misses out the relating dialogue, thus abbreviating the reference. Wertsch called this technique 'abbreviation'. In summary, the adult is scaffolding the learning experiences for the child, first of all helping the child develop understanding and then withdrawing the language prop as s/he acquires the understanding and can do without the extended description related to previous knowledge. The child then shortcuts to that knowledge him/herself.

The everyday environment

Increasingly, the importance of hands-on experiences are recognized as essential precursors of acquiring formal science knowledge and skills. The starting point for the learning of science and engineering is at this early age. This beginning of learning occurs in the immediate environment of the child with the people with whom s/he spends their time. In these locations children witness everyday activities such as cooking, cleaning, washing, various activities with materials such as textiles, wood, clay, as well as identifying and being involved with basic life processes such as moving, breathing, eating, excreting and the human activities associated with the life processes and beyond.

Children are immersed in their environment; built, human constructed or natural such as their village or neighbouring biological phenomena. All these places contain various amounts of technology and biodiversity from a simple cooking vessel being used on an open fire to mobile phones; from natural degeneration to a manicured garden. Moreover, the natural environment is comprised of physical, geological and biological features and elements of these such as rocks, plants and watercourses may be observed. Additionally, the culture and particular uses of science and technology by the community with whom the children live are evident and noticed (Patrick and Tunnicliffe, 2011).

Listening in

In their everyday environment at home, day care, play group, nursery or with other people, these young children hear talk. They hear tones of voices; they hear words and gradually associate a particular set of signs with an object, person or action. It is vital that their adults talk with them and describe what they are doing, what is happening, what things and actions are called as well as expressing emotions using words in addition to actions.

Any of you who have learnt a language that was not your mother tongue may recall that before you can speak the language all you can understand are some of the words gradually; so it is with our early learners. It is so important in learning science that these potential scientists hear the name for plants, animals, physical and chemical phenomena and engineering in action that you see in the everyday. It is important to share the information with them. Ask them questions, point out what you see or name and explain what they point to, find and otherwise show interest in. Remember too that the children hear voices through DVDs and televisions as well as the radio. Some of the programmes they watch and hear are designed for early learners; others are not, but children soon become very aware that language is a part of their world.

Contact with language

Any visit outside the house and when visitors come to call brings children into contact with a variety of signs, including voices with words. In fact, words form a key component of the stimuli in their lives and thus it is very important to provide a child with the optimum help in developing and understanding of the vocabulary. There is an old English saying that 'Children should be seen and not heard'. Indeed, they need to learn words before they speak them, but they listen as the first stage of talking. Just as there is a critical period for language development, so too perhaps these early years are the critical time for science awareness and understanding to be consolidated. If the opportunities are missed an enduring interest and feel for science and engineering may be lacking:

> Children, we now know, need to talk, and to experience a rich diet of spoken language in order to think and learn. Reading, writing and number may be acknowledged as curriculum basics but talk is the true foundation for teaching.
>
> (Alexander, 2008: 9)

Furthermore, it is now accepted that there is an intimate link between language and thought, and thus the cognitive development of a child is affected to a considerable extent by the nature, context and forms of language that s/he hears and uses (Halliday, 1993). Children need to hear adults talking and be talked to by them about what they notice themselves and that which you deem important to bring to their attention; an object, a happening or an action.

Words

Is it important to hear words before a memory can be associated with them and before a child understands what action or object the words stand for? Psychologists have discovered that in later life memories from childhood are recalled when certain words are mentioned. Such words are associated with activities, places, objects and emotions; they also discovered that the memory that was recalled occurred a few months after the time when the word had been acquired, indicating that there was delay between hearing and learning the word and associating it with a related memory. Perhaps, therefore, in the case of learning science and engineering, the hearing of a word associated with an appropriate event is needed before the activity that could form the association. This explains the importance of children hearing the relevant and appropriate words spoken by the adults around them from their earliest years, including the media aimed at the early years, for example programmes such as on CBeebies on the BBC in the UK.

The vocabulary list below includes the words that are frequently relevant to talking science. These are grouped into categories for ease of reading but some of the words fit into several of the categories and hence are repeated; for example, 'full' is a Quantity word but is also a Measurement word. The list is by no means complete; you may well have words that you would add. Select from the lists the words that you think are important for the children to hear and use. Only you can do this because you know the child, the local situation and what has happened before this activity; thus, you can link it with relevant familiar happenings and instances.

However, a word of caution: A child may understand words, but when that word is combined with other letters and sounds that s/he does not recognize, some misunderstanding from an adult's point of view may occur, although to the children their answer or explanation is perfectly obvious. Four-year-old Tilly, from Mauritius but at school in North London, knows a great deal about caterpillars and how they spin cocoons and while inside change into butterflies. When her teaching assistant asked her what caterpillars ate, she replied, 'Rats!' Upon being questioned she answered that cats eat rats, hence she reasoned that the cat-er-pillar was a cat of some sort so it too must eat rats!

Key vocabulary

- *Communications*: Draw, tell, explain, question, answer, write, act, sing, dance, mime, signal

- *Observation words*: Wet, dry, big, little, light, heavy, see-through, transparent, opaque, translucent, uneven, resistance, friction, shadow, reversible, old, new, young, fresh, smell, look, under, side, above, below, bendy, crumples, crumbles, solid, flexible, floppy, squashed, flattened, wobbles, falls, tilts, stretch,   pings, shorter, longer

- *Quantity words*: More, less, empty, full, equal, same as, lighter, heavier, over-flow, particles, lumps

Make them comparative by adding another word, e.g. same or more than – same as this one but more than that one and less than this one but more than this one . . .

- *Measure words*: Time, minute, capacity, weight, mass, measures, non-standard, hand span, finger length, foot length, width, length, height, column, half, estimate, guess, quantity, spoonful, cupful, jugful, drop, fraction, weight-less, less than, more than, bigger than, smaller than, same size

- *Movement words*: Push, pull, force, roll, pick, fall, rise, stop, skid, shuffle, skip, hop, run, swish, swing, squash, shake, absorb, dissolve, disappear, evap-orate, solidify, runny, fast, slow, float, sink, swim, walk, jump, wave, support, hold, grip, gravity, collapse, steady, bubble, still, wobble, bend, curve, crawl, burrow, climb, fly, flap, creep, quickly, sway, hang, glide, tilts

- *Action words*: Push, pull, tear, twist, fold, crunch, squash, flatten, blow, release, scoop, build, burst, on, off, topple, cook, change, drop, watch, listen, smell,
measure, feel, weigh, observe, look, prod, pour, sift, shake, mould, bend, open, stroke, pin, fix, taste, hold, grip, pinch, collide, spray, twirl, heat, cool, dry, wet, switch, join, halve, balance, counter balance, rub, drag, solidify, melt, quick, slow, displace, suspend, hang, attract, push away, repel, spin, stamp

- *Materials/objects words*: Paper, card, clay, plasticine, clay dough, soil, sand, water, liquid, fluids, paints, brushes, pencil, rods, sticks, rulers, crayon, scis-sors, droppers, straws, tissue paper, beakers, cups, plates, bowls, dishes, containers, boxes, lids, trays, spoon, fork, knife, glass, saucepan, pot, kettle, bottle, scales, weights, ice water, fizzy drink, bottle top, pebbles, rocks, salt, sugar, steam, gas, electricity, plug, metre rule, tape measures, string, thread, fabrics, filter paper, kitchen towel, cloth, wool, nylon, silk, cotton, plastic, foil, syringes, tubes, rope, twine, straw, sandpaper, pins, needles, paper clips, scoop, glue, clips, seed tray, stop clock, timer, egg timer, funnel, sieve, brick, cube, block

- *Change words*: Disappear, evaporate, cooked, cold, hot, bigger, smaller, broken, rough, smooth, melt, solidity, expand, contract, empty, fill, heap, flatten, steam, gas, solid, stretches, goes back, mix, change

- *Colours*: Red, orange, yellow, green, blue, indigo, violet, purple, crimson, pale, dark, pink, white, black, ivory, grey, brown, russet, spots, patterned, stripes, blocks, faded, vivid, bright, colourless, transparent

- *Shapes*: Circle, square, triangle, line, egg shaped, rectangle, diamond, rhombus, pentagon, hexagon, globe, cube, dots, base, pyramid, spots, splodges, jagged, symmetrical, piece, part, fragment

- *Position words*: Stand, flat, sideways, upside down, right way up, upright, besides, alongside, together, separate, apart, hole, hollow, top, bottom, under, above, straight, line, curve, bend, back, front, next, underneath, inside, outside, beneath

- *Animal words*: Fish, insect, spider, worm, animal, bones, non-boned, jellyfish, skeleton, water skeleton, vertebrate, invertebrate, bee, wasp, ladybird, daddy longlegs, mosquito, water boatman, dragonfly, fly, midge, bird, seagull, magpie, robin, blue tit, pigeon, blackbird, starling, woodpecker, mouse, frog, toad, tadpole, newt, goldfish, stickleback, tropical fish, sea anemone, barnacle, mollusc, slug, snail, shrimp, horse, cow, sheep, goat, cat, dog, hamster, gerbil, earthworm, woodlouse, beetle, ant, owl, donkey, octopus, zebra, lion, deer, pig, boar, elephant, tiger, leopard, bear, primate, monkey, gorilla, chim- panzee, pheasant, fox, badger, larval, adult, change, metamorphosis, egg, hatch, grow, back, anus, post anal tail, mouth, tentacles, feelers, antennae, exoskeleton, crustacean, dinosaurs, reptiles, snakes, amphibians, fur, spines, wool, prickles, hair, scales, eardrum, ear flaps, tail, teeth, jaws, wings, claws, nails, whiskers, noises, song, bark, sing, chirp, hoot, roar, purr, meow

- *Plant words*: Green, flowers, flowering plant, non-flowering plant, fruit, seed, petals, sepals, leaves, stalk, roots, root hairs, cotyledons, pollen, stamens, anther, filament, stigma, style, sex organs, seedless, cone, spores, capsule, pollination, fruits dispersal, germination, water, split, pod, scent, colour, ripen, bud, drop, deciduous, evergreen, needles, waxy, holly, prickles, potatoes, underground stems, stolons, brambles, nettles, conifers, bushes, twigs, branches, trunk, bark, turgid, flop, upwards, downwards, photosynthesis, geotropic, energy, sun, food, vegetative, reproduction, grafts, cuttings

- *Human words*: Hand, foot, arm, finger, toes, knee, back, front, abdomen, chest, neck, head, skull, bones, blood, bleed, air, breathe, ears, eyes, nose, mouth, chin, teeth, incisors, canine, molars, nails, excrete, urinate, waste, chew, suck, swallow, breathe, respire, beat, digest, hot, cold, temperature, sweat, shiver, goose bumps, reproduce, babies, placenta, care, milk, breast, milk glands, live birth
- *Physical words*: Gas, bubbles, force, lever, machine, ramp, screw, magnet, mirror, image, melt, solidify, state, solid, air
- *Feeling words*: Happy, sad, miserable, beautiful, feeling, care, like, dislike, fear, frightened, brave, courage
- *Senses words*: Smell, hear, see, feel, rough, smooth, sloppy, wet, slimy, prickly, sense
- *Weather words*: Rain, fine, sun, cloudy, hot, cold, chilly, frosty, icy, snowy, humid, clammy, temperature, storms, wind, thunder, lightning, dark, gloomy, breezy, rainbow, muggy, drizzle, heavy rain, light rain, soggy, wet, blowy

Using words

Every time the child is involved in watching or doing an activity with a science or engineering/technology aspect, say words that are relevant to the activity. For example, they may relate to a decorative observation, such as the colour of the dog the child is stroking. They may be action words such as barking, folding or cooking or they may be naming words such as dog, plant, insect or machine.

Communications from the child and using technology

Talking and listening about doing science is not only a one-way transmission from adult to child. The child also has a voice and opinions. Science is about communicating findings, and children usually thoroughly enjoy and instinctively tell an audience about what they have done, what they find exciting and what they think. Communication is not confined to talking at the time of event. Children can draw what they did; drawings are expressed mental models and are sometimes used before an event in order for the child to predict an outcome if s/he does certain things, but more often they are used after an event to try to understand what a child undertook and gleaned from the experience or to try to elect his or her conceptual development in a topic, e.g. Tunnicliffe (2004).

There are two very simple technologies, which are both effective and readily accessible: cameras and video recorders. Children love recording themselves; they can just say what they thought, did and found out, to be played back to themselves and to other children who may then be able to replicate their study, as scientists do. Such recordings can be used in the assessment of their progress or played to parents for them to hear the direct words of their children. Cameras can use film but these do involve the expense of processing. Digital cameras can be a brilliant tool for communication and children can take many, many pictures. One 18-month-old girl in the back of her grandmother's car was able to use a digital camera and took 75 pictures of things she saw during a relatively short journey.

Young children seem able to work out how to use the technology around them, often recreating actions they have observed adults making. The photographs do not have to be uploaded onto computers necessarily but can be looked at on the viewing screen of the camera. Children can be asked to talk about the photographs and choose perhaps a few to be uploaded and printed off. Again, such records can be invaluable if you have to keep a developmental profile. Some places fortunate enough to have useful software such as Purple Mash (www.purplemash.com), a creative online space, or cloud can upload the work of a child into his/her personal folder. Such resources also enable schools to share the work of a child with his/her parents or carers. Children in the early years of school very quickly learn to recognize the symbol for their folder and use their individual log in.

While children do have the opportunity to investigate outside, in some areas this is not as easy and virtual worlds can have their uses. In a way, if a child explores a virtual world first, such as those presented in Simple City (www.2simple.com/simplecity), they can have advance orientation to phenomena such as a zoo, farm or park, three of the sites that Simple City provides, and inquire about 'What?' and 'Where?' before they make the visits. This programme is acting as another form of advance organizer, which is an essential feature of any out of school visits. Using software children can draw their science investigations and observations. The same website offers software such as Create a Story, which enables the child to draw and animate his or her drawing; an animation of a see-saw is the classic example often shown in this programme. There is the facility for the child to have a few words under his or her drawing and add sounds such as a tune as well as his or her commentary. For a pre-writer this is a superb method for having the child develop the art of communicating findings and feelings of science and engineering in his or her life. Video cameras can be used in the same way.

Science journals/folder

Science journals in preschool settings are advocated as tools to support not only children's learning of science but also of literacy; writing about their experiences, like the four-year-old who found a dead bumble bee and was so excited she rushed into the nursery and wrote that she had found a bee, much to the welcome astonishment of her teacher. She suddenly had relevant, personally meaningful content about which she wanted to write and share. Such journals can also be used for assessment (Brenneman & Louro, 2008).

Photo journals

Making a photo album/journal (Katz, 2012) for very young children of photographs that interested them and of what they did from their earliest years, and then going back to it when they are little older and talking about the actions and occasions if they recall it, is a very useful novel longitudinal means of recording and communication. This can give great pleasure to parents, grandparents and others as well as being useful in formal education. It is a useful activity to suggest to parents and carers to do with a child at home.

Drama

Children can communicate their science investigations through drama without any technologies. I once witnessed young children in rural Sri Lanka show what they had found out about growing seeds through a dramatic dance they had composed and subsequently performed for us.

Play, talking, doing and learning

Play defines childhood and is so important to optimal development that it has been recognized and protected by the United Nations Commission for Human Rights in article 31, as the right of every child (Department for Education and Skills, 2004). Increasingly society refers to social justice and one aspect, the rights of children, which is the right of the child to play (Alderson, 2000). It is also accepted wisdom that young children learn crucially important social and emotional skills through play and being formally taught at too early an age (Moyles, 1989) does not allow this essential and critical development. These now accepted rights of the child reinforce that children have the right to play and to structured learning when appropriate.

A word on play

Many practitioners believe in the entitlement to play and a child-centred methodology has emerged (Lancaster & Broadbent, 2003). However, parents may be of the opinion that play is unproductive to the development of their young child, believing that formal schoolwork should prevail to develop learning potential and achievements. It is unfortunate that the word play has many definitions; parents are suspicious of it (Moyles, 1989). Such sentiments led to the statement referring to English formal early learning as two play-arid decades over the closing years of the twentieth century. Many parents believe that a formal method leads to better learning even with the youngest children (Blenkin & Kelly, 1996). Thus the historic stigma of play being regarded as frivolous still looms in the minds of a fraction of parents and educators. It is the experience of many educators who have really worked with children that they apparently respond more effectively to a curriculum concept in formal learning when they have previously experienced it through play.

All kinds of play are essential for learning and development, e.g. Moyles (1989), Broadhead (2006). There are various definitions put forward to designate play; for example, role-play/creative play, physical (outdoor and indoor) play, free/child initiated play, structured adult-led/initiated play. Spontaneous play is a natural activity according to Sheridan (1990: 15), and the orderly developmental sequence is described as:

a) active play;

b) exploratory and manipulative play;

c) imitative play;

d) constructive play or (end product) play;

e) make-believe (or pretend) play; and

f) games with rules.

Moreover, the child moves from infant stage using basic sensory and motor equipment towards more sophisticated and creative communication as a toddler and beyond. However, in this sequence the child is, according to Sheridan (ibid.), dependent on continuing adult encouragement and the provision of suitable toys and other equipment. The encouragement comes through observing and talking to the child, even before s/he can speak, and listening once s/he verbalizes her or his activities, discoveries and emotions. Children rely on adults to help them by providing the scaffolding in the zone of proximal or potential development (Vygotsky, 1962). Materials and activities provided by thoughtful, informed teachers and carers encourage spontaneous play. Play for learning occurs naturally. Furthermore, through planning activities for early learners in their charge the adult is constantly analyzing and observing the learning opportunities and their beneficial achievements while making decisions on necessary adult involvement as to how to move the play forward as the individual needs are met for successful learning and development. Thus, play is more than just the work of children (Broadhead, 2004: 89); it is their self-actualization as they recognize themselves as cognitive beings and proceed to comprehensively explore their world, and their place and response to it.

Health and safety issues

Safe equipment

Check all equipment; do not use items that may hurt the children; for example glass, which may break, or sharp scissors. Eating items is not a good idea unless they are purchased expressly for that purpose and clean utensils are used (no food on the table tops, use clean plates or dry paper napkins and make sure hand washing is scrupulously observed). If you look at moulds have them in a see-through container with a firm lid or sealed with cling film so that spores of the fungi cannot escape to be breathed in.

Animals

Check too if you have animals, particularly mammals, that children are not allergic to them. If some children are, you will have to discuss action with management. Keeping animals in class is a valuable activity because it enhances observational skills and can instill attitudes of care and welfare.

Mealworms are ideal animals to keep. They live on bran or similar food and need a piece of potato or apple for moisture every so often. If the container is small they will need cleaning every so often and a large holed sieve can be used to separate the substrate, which needs replacing, and the animals. Mealworms develop from an egg into larvae, and then a chrysalis from which they emerge in their adult form as beetles. The eggs are very small but you may see some as you clean them out. You can study the whole life story of an insect that undergoes a complete change or metamorphosis to the adult form, as do butterflies, frogs and other amphibians. Children can feel the power of another living thing on their hand. All you need is a small see-through plastic aquarium with a lid or a piece of cling film with a few holes punched in it stretched across the top.

Do take advice from the RSPCA or CLEAPSES before keeping other animals. The Association for Science Education publishes a book called *Be Safe!* that contains helpful advice and is a useful reference document. For example, the book points out that terrapins can carry Salmonella, meaning that children should wash their hands when they have touched animals or been digging in the soil.

Conclusion

The take away message is that children need to observe and take part in activities that are science and engineering in the everyday world. They need to hear the words and conversations about such phenomena long before they acquire the facility of talking for themselves. These early experiences are critical in the development of a feel for, and understanding of, science and engineering in their lives and it is important to recognize those activities in the context of the culture in which they occur.

4 Living things – ourselves

Summary

Human beings are animals. We belong to the large group of animals that have three layers to their body development. All these animals, from true worms up to humans, have a through gut that begins with an entry, a mouth, through which food and water enters and finishes with an exit, the anus, through which waste leaves. We have bones so are vertebrates, and are warm blooded with hair and give birth to live babies, which feed on milk; we are mammals.

Key words

Chordates, mammals, vertebrae, notochord, primate, tetrapod, digits, pentadactyl, limb, opposable thumb, electrolytes, deciduous teeth, stereoscopic vision, bipedal, placental mammals, quadrupeds, metamorphosis.

Big ideas

Body plan round a tube

Animals from earthworms upwards have a tube through the middle of their body from the front to the back end. A model of the three-layered body can be simply made. You need a tube to represent the outside of the body, something to fill the body cavity and something to represent the through gut between the organs. Use a cardboard tube, such as a toilet-roll tube, pack it with tissue then insert a plastic drinking straw through the middle of the tissue so each end of the straw is left sticking out. The straw represents the gut, the tissue is the organs and the space they occupy is the body cavity while the outside of the body is represented by the card tube wall.

Excess fluid in mammals leaves the body as urine, a solution of wastes and other chemicals. This leaves the body by a separate exit in all mammals, unlike in birds and reptiles that have one opening (a cloaca) for waste, which in birds is uric acid, a white paste-like substance. This is different from two-layered animals such as jellyfish, whose food goes in and waste comes out of the same opening. In fact, there is a super ordinate category of chordates, which all have a notochord. This is a supple rod-shaped form running down the topside of the animal's body. It is found in all chordates in their embryos and in more 'advanced' animals it develops into the spine of bones called vertebrae. In the earliest of chordates the notochord, made up of cells, was a very straight structure to which muscles were attached. The remains of the notochord structure form part of the discs between the vertebrae in our spine. An animal that has a notochord but no backbone (hence no skeleton) is a lancelet. Such animals are chordates but not verte-brates, whereas all vertebrates are chordates.

Primates

The vertebrates are in turn divided into those with a jaw, like we humans, and those without, like lampreys and hagfish. We humans are mammals and in the subcategory of primates. We are tetra pods – four-limbed animals like all land-living vertebrates (although you cannot see the limbs in snakes on the outside) that share the same basic vertebrate skeleton pattern. Human limbs, and hands and feet, are in the basic pentadactyl pattern. We have five digits, fingers and toes. These are unspecialized and primates have the ability to make their thumb and first finger meet; this opposable thumb enables us to pick things up. Other primates such as chimpanzees can also do this. In fact they can use their toes too.

Basic animal needs

Like all animals, humans have basic needs – for food, water, shelter, protection and to meet a mate. We all have the same physiological process of respiration, taking oxygen into our bodies through breathing or respiratory movements and exhaling waste prod-ucts of cellular registration, which is carbon dioxide. This is an excretory process as is voiding urine and fecal material. Sweating is also an excretory process. Sweat contains some chemicals, particularly sodium, chloride, potassium, magnesium, calcium, phosphate and bicarbonate, known as electrolytes. Sodium and chloride are the major electrolytes lost in sweat. A sodium ion is positively charged and chloride is negatively charged. They are vital to life because they enable cells to carry electrical charges, which are needed for nerve transmission and muscle action. Kidneys regulate the amount of electrolytes in our body and replace them when lost to keep the body stable.

When there are not enough electrolytes, like when fluids containing them are lost in, for example, excessive sweating, vomiting or diarrhoea, the body cannot work and this loss of fluids with the electrolytes can be fatal. Health and sports drinks often advertise that they contain electrolytes.

Body temperature

Mammals have a constant body temperature and are thus called warm blooded. The human core body temperature is about 37°C, 98.6°F The extremities, fingers and toes, feet and hands, elbows and knees are cooler than the inside core of the body. The temperature a human body can survive dropping to before dying of cold is 27°C, while the highest internal temperature the body can withstand before death is 43°C. Humans try to keep their body within this range by the type of clothing they wear, what they do and adapting to their environment. The body tries to regulate its temperature by sweating when it is hot or shivering when it is cold. As the sweat evaporates from the skin it cools the blood underneath and shivering produces heat from the muscular action to warm the blood. Dehydration when the body stops sweating can be fatal.

Mammal and special human features

As mammals we have hair and two sets of teeth, which are not all the same. Adults have molars, premolars, canines and incisors. Humans have what we call 'milk teeth'; 20 in total, 10 in each jaw. There are two incisors, one canine and two premolars in each half jaw (humans, like other mammals, only have one bone in their lower jaw). These teeth start appearing from about six months of age. The incisors, the front teeth, appear first. These are usually the first to be replaced by permeate teeth, which will have replaced all of the primary teeth by the age of ten years, starting to appear from the age of six years onwards. As another commonality with other mammals, humans also have a diaphragm across the middle of the body cavity and this assists in our respiratory or breathing movements.

Permanent teeth

By age of 12 years or so children have replaced all the milk or deciduous teeth with their permanent teeth, of which there are 32. The last four molars right at the back of the jaw are called wisdom teeth. In some adults they never erupt, so they only have 28 teeth. Teeth are used to obtain and prepare food for the digestive process and in some mammals for defence; the fangs of tigers for example. Mammals have different teeth for different purposes. The front teeth, incisors, are used for nibbling. The canines, the sharp teeth, are used for stabbing and biting. Premolars and molars, the big teeth at the back, are used for chewing and grinding up food into smaller parts. Teeth reflect the main diet of their owners, so the meat eaters have canines like fangs for stabbing and holding prey and shearing teeth for cutting. Plant eaters, herbivores, have large molars for grinding plant material and incisors for nibbling grass.

Two legged and stereoscopic vision

Gradually in vertebrate evolution the bones that made up the lower jaw have become part of the inner ear, the maleus, incus and stapes bones. We are upright so are called bipedal, like birds. Unlike our close primate relatives the hole at the base of the human skull is underneath so the head balances on the body, which is upright, with the front exposed to the world, not hidden underneath as in four-legged animals. We look straight ahead. Humans also have stereoscopic vision; we see things in three dimensions and can judge distances, essential when leaping from branch to branch. We walk with two legs, which leave the other two limbs, arms, free to use tools and do things.

Growing babies

We grow our babies inside us, so babies have to leave the body of their mother and subsequently feed on milk produced by the mother. Other mammals (warm blooded animals with hair) are like humans and keep the egg that grows into the baby inside their body in a special place reserved for growing offspring. In this place there is a special fluid around the growing baby in an amniotic sac, the membranes, which have to break to let the baby out. These are placental mammals; animals that start life in fluid. When grown and ready to leave its mother, the baby is pushed out from the uterus into the world where it takes its first breath of air. Using the strong muscles that open the uterus opening, cervix first, the mother pushes the baby down the birth canal. This is more difficult in humans as we walk upright and the canal has become curved. Quadrupedal or four-legged mammals have a straight birth canal.

Inside its mother the developing baby is fed through a tube connecting to a special organ, the placenta. This takes food in the form of chemicals and the oxygen the baby needs from the mother's blood into the baby's blood, to be carried round its body to the cells that need the chemicals. Waste chemicals are removed in the same way.

Helpless newborn

Newborn humans are helpless and need looking after for a number of years, as in other primates. Young orangutans for instance are looked after for the first four years of their lives, but human young need to be cared for even longer. Human babies cannot move around when they are born and have got be carried about until they learn to walk, usually at over a year old. Some babies crawl very effectively before walking. Young humans resemble the adult although much smaller and their head is much bigger in proportion to the rest of their body. New babies cannot control their bladder and anal sphincters so human babies in many countries wear nappies to catch the waste. Sometimes the baby's tube to its stomach gets full and some milk regurgitates and comes out of its mouth. Parents and carers look after all these things for helpless babies.

Gradual change in form as humans grow up

Young humans grow gradually so have an incomplete metamorphosis, unlike for example, tadpoles and caterpillars, which look very different as young in comparison to their adult form and undergo a complete change (metamorphosis).

Language and abstract thought

Humans have language and abstract thought to a much greater extent than other animals. Human language acquisition is a complicated process and apparently more complex than in other species that have a communication system.

Talking and doing

The following activities aim to provide young children with hands-on relevant experiences, which, together with the dialogue constructed around them, will provide some foundation understanding of the human form. Providing hands-on activities introduces the concept that we humans are similar to yet different from other animals.

 ## Me!

Draw the outline of a child's body on a large piece of flip chart paper, or piece of light-coloured sugar or construction paper. Write the names of the main external parts of the body that the children need to learn on sticky notes.

Perhaps use these words: head, neck, ears, eyes, mouth, nose, hair, chin, cheek, chest, abdomen, back, shoulder, elbow, wrists, hand, fingers, upper leg, hip, lower leg, ankle, foot, toes, heel.

Name the parts

Ask the children to name a part of the human body. When they say the name give them the Post-it with that name written on and invite them to attach it to the body.

You could have them stick the name note onto the appropriate body part of a child if you think that a suitable task.

What can I do?

Ask the children what they can do, using some of the questions below:

- How do they move from place to place?
- How do they pick things up? Put on their clothes?
- How do they eat things? Drink things?
- How do they communicate with each other and you?

Me and other animals

You could use the following questions to discover what the children know about animals:

- What other animals do the children know?
- Have you photographs, pictures or models such as realistic plastic molded toy animals for them to talk about?
- Is the shape of these animals like a human?
- Have they the same number of legs?
- Have they a mouth that can be seen? Do they have lips? A tongue?
- Do they have teeth? Are their teeth different like human teeth? (Reptiles like crocodiles have teeth that are all the same shape.)
- Do their eyes point forward like ours?
- Have they fur or other body covering
- How does each animal move around?
- How does each animal get its food?
- How does each animal drink?
- How does each animal communicate?

Make an 'Other Animals and Me' chart – the one opposite is a suggestion.

Hole through the middle

Have some card tubes, some tissue paper or tissues and some bendy or straight straws.

Show the children that you can make a model of an animal's body, a three-layered animal such as earthworms, cats, fish, beetles and us.

Action	Me	Cat	Dog	Bird e.g. Pigeon	Earthworm	Butterfly	Fish	Beetle
Where do they live?	Land	Land	Land	Air and land	Surface and in soil	Air	Water Sea and fresh water	Everywhere! On plants, in ground, under stones, in food
How do they move?	Walk and run	Walk	Walk	Flies	Moves itself with its body, pushes against ground and bristles	Flies	Swims	Crawl, sometimes fly if they have wings
What do they use to move?	Two legs	Four legs	Four legs	Wings in the air, legs on land	Its body in touch with soil	Wings in air	Fins and tail	Six legs, wings for beetles that fly
How do they eat/ obtain food?	Use hands and tools	Uses mouth	Mouth	Beak/ mouth	Mouth	They drink nectar with their tongue	Mouth	Mouth parts

Put the straw through the tube and tell the children that this is to represent the gut, where food goes in at one end and waste food such as fibre and seeds comes out at the other. The body is built around this tube. Put tissue between the straw and the tube wall and they have made a simple model of the body plan.

Thumbless

Have a few items that can be picked up in a tray such as a pencil, a plastic mug, a small book, a spoon, a piece of paper and pieces of string.

Ask the children what each item is for. How do they pick them up from the tray? What part of their body do they usually use for this? Do they use fingers and thumb in a different way? Can they pick up as easily with either hand?

Then tell them they have to pretend not to be a primate, and thus have no opposable thumb. What is an opposable thumb?

Ask the children to move their thumbs away from the next finger and make an 'O' shape by touching the tip of their first finger with the tip of the thumb. This is the opposable thumb.

Now suggest they try to pick up the items without being able to do this thumb-to-finger movement; now can they pick up the things they picked up just before?

How do other animals, such as cats, pick things up?

Using one eye

Put a ruler at the edge of a table so most of it is sticking out.

Can the children touch the tip of the ruler standing just over an arm's length away?

Then ask them to close one eye and try again. What happens? We need to use two eyes to judge distances. Some people only use one eye at a time and they learn to compensate in judging distances, for example when pouring out a drink into a cup. Try that too with two eyes and then only one.

Teeth

Use mirrors. Can the children see their teeth? What colour are they? Are they all the same shape? What are the edges of their teeth like? Are the teeth all the same? What different shapes can they see?

Which teeth do they use for what? What action with food?

Ask them to pretend to eat an apple. Which teeth do they use to bite into the apple first?

What food do they use their front teeth, the nibbling teeth, for?

When they chew food like bread or pieces of meat, which teeth do they use?

What does their tongue do when they are eating food?

How do they drink something? What happens if they use a straw?

Breathing movements

When they are sitting still what parts of them are still moving? Ask them to sit and think about it.

They might realize that their chest is moving up and down. These are the breathing movements to draw air in and then push it out with the water from their lungs.

Breathing rates

Ask the children: Do you always breathe the same times a minute? Is a breathing rate always the same?

Ask the children to jump up and down on the spot for a minute or some other activity, then ask if their breathing rate is different. Why do they think they have changed?

What else did they notice when they were active? Do they change colour in their face? Do they feel the same temperature as when they began moving or do they feel colder or hotter?

Balance

We humans have to balance on two legs. Not always easy!

What happens when you stand on one leg? Why do we wobble sometimes? What are we naturally trying to do?

Ask the children to stand on their two legs and look down. What do they see?

Ask them to balance on one leg, then look down; what do they see? Is the foot on which they are standing under them in the same place or have they shifted the weight of their body over it? Ask one child to watch another stand on two feet then stand on one foot. Does the standing child move his or her body to stay balanced on one leg?

Ask children to try bending down to touch their toes. What do they do? Now try doing it next to a wall; they can't, because we have to move back a bit, moving the weight of our body out over our hips and legs so we don't topple over.

Walking

What part of our body do we use when we walk? Ask the children to walk up and down. What parts of them do they use? Which parts touch the floor? How would they walk on a slippery surface? Why would they slide, perhaps? (There is little or no friction.)

What do they do with each foot as it touches the floor? They push – this is a force! How do they change legs when walking? Where does the leg that is going to touch the floor start off? The leg swings forward and takes the weight of the body and then the other leg swings forward as the one with the foot on the ground pushes the body forward. How does the body move as the legs change sides to touch the floor?

Babies

Have some pictures of newborn babies, babies crawling, a toddler holding on to a walker, a young child running about, a nine-year-old, a teenager and a grown up.

All the same?

Ask the children: What is the difference between a new baby and a grown up?

Are you like a baby now?

What is the difference between a new baby and the children? How do they eat, move, and communicate?

Make a table

You can alter this to suit you and your children and the categories according to age of children; perhaps insert toddler or older preschool children and teenagers?

How and what?	New baby	Me	Grown up
Food	Milk		Everything
Drink	Milk, water		Water, tea, coffee, juice, other things
Way of eating	Given it by mother from her body or by her or someone else from a bottle or spoon for water		Fingers, knives, forks and spoons
Moves	Carried		Walks, runs
Talks	Gurgles and cries		Uses speech
Sleeps	A lot		Usually at night for 6–8 hours
Clothes	Nappies, all-in-one suits		Suits, trousers, dresses, underwear, etc.
Shape	Head big Flat chest Downy hair		Head much smaller Body bigger Females have two breasts sticking out of chest Lot of hair on head (unless bald)

Where do human babies grow?

Ask the children: Where do babies come from? How can you tell if a baby is growing inside its mother? Can you tell as soon as it starts to grow?

Preparing for baby

What do mothers and fathers need to get ready for a baby so they have all the baby needs before it is born? Ask the children what they think the baby will need. Where will it sleep? How will it be taken outside and for a walk? What will it wear? Cut out pictures of baby things and ask the children for what they are used. Perhaps you could make a mobile from cut out pictures of baby things.

Waste from babies

You could ask the children about the baby's waste products. What about things that come out of the baby? What if it has had too much milk and the tube to the stomach is filled up to overflow? What about the wastes that all mammals produce? What sort of things do humans use to cope with these things that come from the baby's body?

Feeding baby

How will it be fed? What sort of things does a mother need? How does a baby let the people looking after it know that it is hungry? That something is not right? What else do children think or know that new babies have?

All the same or not?

Are we humans all the same or are we different? Ask the children to look around at the people in the room. Are they the same in any way? Are they different? Are all the people the same height?

Small and large

Ask someone to identify the smallest, the tallest. Has everyone the same hair colour? Has everyone the same eye colour? Has everyone the same skin colour? Has everyone the same number of arms and legs? Fingers? Eyes, noses, mouth? Talk about differences. Do they happen in other animals such as cats or birds?

Outcomes

By working through these activities as relevant to the children with whom you are working, bearing in mind their age and previous experiences as well as the context in which you and the children are interacting, these early learners should gain a basic understanding of the biology of humans and some shared features of mammals together with some unique human features.

5 Other living things – animals

Summary

Although technically humans are animals, they are but one kind of animal. This chapter discusses differences between humans and other animals; how different groups eat, move and keep warm, for example. It introduces children to mammals and considers the similarities and the differences between themselves and other animals. Activities grouping everyday animals, e.g. birds, mammals, insects and annelids are introduced to highlight the differences and similarities of various animal groups. There are also activities to find out how other kinds of animals carry out the essential life activities that we humans have such as eating, feeling, moving, having babies and growing up. This chapter suggests children group animals using toy models, giving reasons for the match; for example, parents and offspring. This chapter also introduces the big idea that some animals change to adult forms gradually, an incomplete metamorphosis, while others have a complete change in form, a complete metamorphosis.

> ### Key words
>
> Cells, metamorphosis, vertebrates, invertebrates, digits, ligaments, muscles, bilateral symmetry, radial symmetry, insects, amphibians, reptiles, dinosaurs, arthropods, molluscs, millipedes, centipedes, echinoderms, sexual dimorphism, carnivores, herbivores, omnivores, predator, prey, food chains.

Big ideas

Made of units called cells

Animals are made up of many cells. The adult body has changed from that of the young animal. This change is called metamorphosis and can be complete, as in for example butterflies, moths and beetles, or incomplete, as in locusts, dogs and cats, where the young are small versions of the adult with a few adult features not yet developed.

Animals catch food

Animals cannot make their food like plants so have to find it instead; some animals live on other animals and are called parasites. They take their food ready made from what another animal has obtained itself, such as tapeworms, which live in the gut of another animal and absorb some of the food it has digested.

Symmetry

Animals are either radially symmetrical, like jellyfish, or bilaterally symmetrical, like sea anemones and coral. Other animals are bilaterally symmetrical, for example cats, birds, butterflies and worms. One side is a mirror image of the other. Some echino- derms (starfish and sea urchins) look radially symmetrical on the outside but inside they are not. They have developed the radial form from a bilaterally symmetrical ancestor. Sea cucumbers, another kind of echinoderm, are very obviously bilaterally symmetrical.

Specialized cells

Animals have bodies with the cells developed into different parts, such as muscles and ligaments, nerves that send messages and sense organs that sense what the world outside their bodies is like. Animals have to have something against which muscles can push that and also gives a shape to their body: a skeleton. Skeletons are either internal, made of fluid like earthworms and the jellyfish group or outside the body like the arthropods, crabs, insects and the spider groups. An inside skeleton is nearly always made of bone except for the very primitive animal with a notochord.

Hole through the body – the gut

Most animals have a through gut with internal parts such as a stomach. Food taken into the gut is first broken down mechanically by teeth or some other mechanism (like knives and forks), so food enters the mouth of a human in small bits and is then broken down further by chemicals, into its smallest chemical parts. The chemicals are what the body needs to build new cells and organs and to provide energy to keep the cells working. After the chemicals pass through the wall of the special part of the gut the remaining waste has water taken away and what is left is excreted from the end of the gut through a special hole, the anus, whose opening and closing is controlled by muscles. In some animals the anus and the urethra, the opening for urine to leave the body, are combined. Such a shared waste exit is called a cloaca. This is found in fish, amphibians, reptiles and their descendants, birds. It is also the opening in these animals used for reproduction. The cell walls of these animals are not made of cellulose and are not rigid with a definite shape like plant cells.

Animals with bones, the vertebrates

Animals are divided into two main groups: the boned or vertebrates, and non-boned or invertebrates. All vertebrates have a post-anal tail and a basic vertebrate skeleton pattern. Ligaments attach bones to each other, with muscles also attached to the bones that pull and push to bring about movement. The basic body pattern of vertebrates has a front end with a spine and a skull, ending in tail bones at the other end with the rest of the backbone linking them together in between.

There are two girdles that join the limbs to the rest of the skeleton. The first, at the front nearest the head, is called the pectoral or chest girdle, and the second, at the back, the pelvic girdle. Each has two limbs, with a basic arrangement of one bone joined to two bones at a joint, knee or elbow. These two bones, lower arm or leg, are then linked with a number of smaller bones, forming the wrist or ankle. These each have connected to them five bones, metacarpals or metatarsals attached to which are the digits, five on each appendage usually consisting of three small bones. The basic pastern is modified in some animals that walk on two toes such as pigs, three toes such as rhinos, or one toe such as horses. Other vertebrates such as cats and dogs walk on pads formed from all five digits. Vertebrates are bilaterally symmetrical; cut down the middle from head to tail one side is the mirror image of the other.

Mammals (except seals) have earflaps, which in most mammals move in the direction of a sound.

Grouping boned animals

Vertebrates are grouped according to their body covering or number of limbs, for example. Fish are cold blooded and their bodies are covered with scales. They live in water, have fins and lay their eggs in water. Amphibians have moist skins and mate, lay eggs and begin life living in water, but some members, such as frogs, come out of the water onto land as they grow up and change to the adult form, but have to live in moist places, often returning to ponds. They obtain some of the oxygen they need from the layer of water on their skin, as they do when living in water. Reptiles such as snakes, tortoises and lizards have dry scaly skins, live on land, and lay eggs with leathery coverings in which the developing baby is in its own private pond on land. Some turtles live in the sea but return to the land to lay their eggs. Dinosaurs were reptiles. Birds are the direct descendants of reptiles and still have scaly skin on their legs but the scales on the rest of the body have evolved into feathers. The adapted scales, feathers, cover their body except for their beak (and the top of the head in birds that eat carrion, such as vultures).

Birds

Birds are warm blooded and their young develop in an egg. Birds' eggs have a shell and, as they are warm-blooded animals, the eggs have to be kept warm while the baby develops. Hence, one of the parents sits on them until they hatch. Chicks, like baby reptiles, have an egg tooth on their beak, which helps them crack the eggshell. They have two legs, the front limbs modified as wings and they fly. Mammals have a body covering of hair, differentiated teeth, and developed inside the mother effectively with structures similar to those in an egg but with no outer covering.

Animal without bones, invertebrates

Invertebrates, like vertebrates, are made of lots of cells but unlike the vertebrates they have no bones and therefore no backbone. Most of the animals in the world (about 97 per cent) are invertebrates. There are over 30 groups or phyla of different kinds of animals without backbones. The simplest ones are the sponges, whose cells are grouped together but are undifferentiated. Next are the cnidarians (previously called coelenterates). These are jellyfish and sea anemones, groups that are radially symmetrical. The body parts are arranged in a circular form, so they can be cut across the middle in any direction and the two halves are still mirror images.

The rest of the invertebrate groups

These are the annelids, the earthworm and leeches group and, the largest group of boneless or invertebrate animals is the arthropods, which have an outside or exoskeleton. They in turn are subdivided into subgroups of myriopoda, which are divided into centipedes and millipedes. A water-living group of animals with hard outsides (an exoskeleton) is the crustaceans (lobsters, crabs and water fleas). The insect class, spiders and scorpions (the arachnids) are the other main groups of arthropods. Other invertebrate groups are the mollusca, which include snails with real shells, slugs and other squids and octopi. The other big group is that of the starfish, sea urchins and sea cucumber group; the echinoderms.

Arthropods have an outer skeleton like the surface of beetles. All insects have six pairs of legs. Those with wings have two pairs (hardened to form wing cases in beetles, like ladybirds) and these, like the legs, are on the second part of their body. They have a pair of antennae. Caterpillars only have three pairs of true legs too. The rest of the appendages on their body are supports, called drop legs. Arachnids, the spider groups, have two parts of their body and four pairs of soft legs coming from the front part of the body. Crustaceans, the crab groups, have two pairs of feelers or antennae and more than three pairs of soft legs. Molluscs, snails and slugs have one large muscular foot. Earthworms, belonging to the annelid phyla, have many segmented body parts and have no limbs. These animals are bilaterally symmetrical; one side is the mirror image of the other.

Most invertebrates or non-boned animals are bilaterally symmetrical. Earthworms are some of the simplest animals and their bodies are made of segments. They have a front end, live in moist surroundings and can often be found under stones. The largest group of invertebrates are the arthropods, with an outside or exoskeleton and jointed legs, specialized mouthparts, jointed bodies and compound eyes, made up of many small lenses. They are the largest group of animals alive on the planet and most are small, apart from a few, like some crabs, that are much larger (there is a large one in the Natural History museum in Oxford).

Hard outsides

The groups of arthropods are crustaceans, insects, millipedes and centipedes. Most arthropods belong to one of three groups: crustaceans (such as crabs, shrimps, water fleas and land-living woodlice), insects (such as butterflies, beetles or flies) and arachnids. Crustaceans have two pairs of antennae and more than six legs, usually ten or more. Most live in water, but some, like woodlice, live on land but in moist places. Insects have three parts to their body (head, thorax and abdomen), one pair of antennae and six legs, three on each side attached to the middle of their three-part body. The millipedes and centipedes with long segmented bodies have many legs. Millipedes have two pairs of legs on most of their body segments, whereas centipedes only have one. They have simple eyes and mouthparts under the head. Millipedes and centipedes are often seen under stones.

How arthropods develop – three stages after the egg

Most arthropods start as a small egg that develops into a larva and then changes into an adult with a metamorphosis. Sometimes, as with grasshoppers and locusts, this is gradual; in other arthropods such as beetles and butterflies they have a dramatic change from a larva, like a caterpillar, through a pupa or change stage into the adult form, which is very different to look at, usually with wings. Even so if the larvae have legs they have three pairs. The other appendages on, for example, a caterpillar, are false legs.

5.1 Caterpillar, young stage of a butterfly or moth.

5.2 This snail has a muscular foot, a mouth and a hole at its side through which it breathes.

One foot – molluscs: slugs and snails

Molluscs have unregimented bodies, an internal or external shell, which is secreted by the mantle, a special mollusc organ. Molluscs also have a single muscular foot like a snail or tentacles like an octopus. The snails and slugs have a tooth-like structure called the radial in their mouth, which scrapes food off surfaces. Many soft herbaceous plants in gardens have holes bored in them or their flowers and leaves completely eaten (often leaving the stalks) by slugs and snails.

Water-living snails obtain their oxygen from water through two sets of gills. Some water snails have a lung and they can be seen at the surface of the water breathing. Land slugs and snails have lungs and the air enters through a hole in their side that you can see. The bodies of molluscs that children will see most are slugs and snails. Slugs have a head like a snail but their insides or organs are not in a lump covered by a shell.

Echinoderms – starfish and sea urchin group

Most starfish and sea urchins that belong to this group and are probably the most familiar to young children, look radially symmetrical with several arms (five or more, mostly grouped two left – one middle – two right) radiating from a centre. The body is made up of five equal segments, each containing an identical set of the internal organs. Echinoderms have no heart, brain or eyes. The mouth is on the underside and their anus on top in soft echinoderms. They have tentacles called tube feet with suction pads, which can easily be seen on the underside of starfish 'arms'. The tube feet work like suction feet being controlled by fluid in the animal's circulatory system, resulting in a suction effect. Movement is slow!

Sexual dimorphism – males and females look different

Sexual dimorphism is when male and female animals are very different in their looks. Peacock males are very colourful with flamboyant tail feathers whereas the female peahen is smaller and brown without the large tail of impressive feathers. Mallard duck females are brown but the male has a metallic green head covering and different browns on the rest of his body. On the other hand, swans look very similar. Children need to consider the special characteristics of each kind of animal, and then be able to distinguish between adults and young, e.g. kitten and cat, chick and hen, and between males and female adults such as cow and bull, ram and ewe, African lion with a mane and the lioness with no mane, domestic hen and cockerel.

Feeding

All animals feed on living things, ready-made food, either directly by catching another animal or eating their food where it grows, e.g. plants. Some animals specialize in eating other animals that are dead, such as vultures, and these are called scavengers. If animals eat only other animals they are called carnivores, if they eat plants only they are called herbivores and if they eat both plants and animals they are called omnivores.

Finding meat to eat

Animals that hunt their food are called predators and kill their prey. Other carnivores such as vultures eat dead animals that they find. Some animals such as blowflies lay their eggs on decaying meat so that their babies (the larvae or young stage called maggots) have food to eat when they hatch from their egg. Animals try not to be caught by other animals hunting for food and have evolved various mechanisms to avoid this, e.g. camouflage. Hunters too have evolved ways of not being seen so they can creep up on prey; for example lions creep up (usually groups of lionesses do the hunting) and then run very fast at the last minute and jump on their prey. Lions suffocate their prey by grabbing the throat and pulling the animal to the ground. Insects such as the praying mantis are camouflaged to look like a leaf or two but when an insect comes near quickly put out their front legs, catch the insect and bite off its head. Spiders spin a web in which insects become trapped.

Meat eating mammals

Mammals that eat animals have specialized teeth. The canines are like fangs positioned on either side of both upper and lower jaw and have developed as cutting and shearing teeth called carnassials for tearing meat. The other back teeth chew the food. Watch a dog or cat chew a bone and you can see it using the side teeth.

Plant eaters

Plant eaters have flattened back teeth for grinding plant material and their jaw moves from side to side. Their front teeth, incisors, are flat and adapted for nibbling. Rodents such as squirrels have incisors that are orange and adapted for gnawing. These continually grow. Sheep for instance have no upper front teeth and a horny pad covers the area. They have a gap called a diastema where the fang teeth would be. They can pull grass through this gap with their tongue and then cut it with their front teeth against this pad.

Other animals eating

Some insects such as butterflies have tongues like straws so they can suck up nectar from flowers; humming birds have similar beaks for the same reason. Other insects such as mosquitoes or greenfly have mouthparts that pierce the skin of plants or animals and then have pump mechanisms so they can suck up fluids. Birds have beaks that are adapted for the food they eat. Flamingos have downward-curving beaks for filtering food from mud and water they scoop up into their mouths. Woodpeckers have beaks like chisels so that they can peck their way into tree trunks to find grubs to eat. Other animals that live in water, like sea anemones, stay still while attached to a rock and wait for water currents; they then extend into the current and catch food that passes by.

Learning what animals are called

Children have to learn the animals that are instances of a concept. 'Cat', 'dog', 'elephant' and 'aardvark', for example are instances of the concept 'animal'. Commonly around the world the use of the term 'animal' by young children is restricted either to mammals or to vertebrates, of which the prototypic member is a mammal. Young children who are inexperienced in seeing a variety of mammals call an unfamiliar animal by the name of any animal that it resembles. For example, 'dog', having hair and four legs could be the name given to any similar animal, such as a cat or cow.

Changes in form – growing up

Recognizing metamorphosis, the different forms of the same kind of animal in different stages of its life and growing up are also problematic for children. Young children often consider intuitively that physically smaller animals are at an earlier stage in their life history than larger and similar specimens, even when the animals are of different species. Children have to learn to recognize the stages of the different form that an animal may assume during its life, like caterpillar, pupa and adult butterfly or tadpole and frog. They also have to learn the different members of the same group of animal, for example that dogs, cats, squirrels and lions are all in the mammals group and in the cat group there are a number of different kinds of cats such as domestic cats, tigers, lions and snow leopards.

Talking and doing

Select from the following activities, according to the age and experience of your charges, from the simplest to the more complex, those that your children would benefit from, to consolidate their existing knowledge. They will learn to recognize the distinct animal forms, behaviours and ways of feeding and growing up. Some of the animals may not have been seen first-hand but the resources of the Internet and other media, as well as field trips to zoos and nature centres, can provide visual interactions with a wide variety of animals. Through these activities children may learn to recognize different animals and name them and their features and be able to justify their naming of specimens.

What animals?

What animals do the children know about? Can they identify animals from their shape or from pictures in books or on toys and household objects such as starfish in bathrooms?

Real everyday animals

Introduce the names of any everyday animal. Young children will name animals when they first start noticing that a) there are animals and b) there are different kinds, often applying this first name to lots of different animals. Any object seen in the air is a bird, if that were the name of the first air borne object they were told, and an animal on the ground is a worm if an earthworm was the first such animal they saw.

Bilateral and radial symmetrical animals

Cut out some circles. Draw an oblong and put a head at one end and a tail at the other. Put legs down each side. Draw a line down the middle of the oblong and across the circle so it passes through the middle. Ask the children, 'What is there one of on either side of the line? What has happened to the head and tail shapes?' They are divided in two. Draw a line across the middle of the circle so it bisects the other line at right angles. Draw a line across the oblong with bit sticking out. Ask the children what they see in each half now. Are both halves the same? They should realize 'yes' for the circle but 'no' for the oblong.

Take a flat unbreakable mirror and place on lines across each shape in turn. Ask the children what they see. They should always see a mirror image if a mirror is put down the middle of the oblong from the top end to the bottom. What do the children think they will see? Each side looks like the other but not if you put the mirrors across the shape along the midpoint. One end has a head and the other a tail.

Let them play with the mirror on the shapes and see for themselves.

Find pictures of animals and use a mirror to see if one side looks like the view in the mirror. Only animals like jellyfish and sea anemones have this property. Let the children describe which animals are the same wherever the mirror is placed across them and which have two halves. What about people?

Making half a teddy whole – bilateral symmetry

Have a toy teddy bear and cut out a matching paper shape. Fold the paper teddy shape down the middle so that you see half a teddy. Put it on top of the real teddy and ask the children what they see. Lay the teddy on top of the open shape. Ask the children where a line has to be so you can get a mirror image of teddy that makes him look whole.

If you have a long enough mirror try putting the mirror across teddy and see what is in the mirror image. Does this make a whole teddy? Put the mirror on the topside of teddy from his head to his feet between his legs and look again. Using a beany baby animal makes it easier to do this if you can not find a big enough mirror.

What is it?

When you see an animal ask children what they call it. What makes them know it is that kind of animal? Is it the shape of the body or the number of legs? Where it is moving – is it walking on land, flying in the air or moving in the water with its fins? Point out that birds have feathers and a beak and wings. Dogs have hair coats and bark whereas cats have fur, are smaller and meow or purr.

Is it a boned or non-boned animal?

It is easy recognize that some animals such as dogs and cats are vertebrates or bone animals, because their tail doesn't always cover their back end and their anus or waste food outlet hole can easily be seen. How many other animals do the children see that has a tail like that?

Moving ears

Watch a dog, cat or other pet mammal and see if its ears move. Which way do they move? When do they move?

Feet

Look at different animals' feet. Do all animals have feet like ours? How many do they have? How many legs?

Tip toe

Do the four-legged animals the children see around walk on five toes like dogs and cats, one toe like a horse or two toes like a pig? How many toes do children walk on when walking on tip toe like these animals do? Their heel is off the ground so walking on tip toe is effectively what these animals are doing.

Two feet

What sort of feet do the two-legged animals have? Do they walk on their toes? How can you find out?

Birds' feet

Have the children seen birds that live in water? Do they know the names of any water birds? What are their feet like? Why? What do they eat? Where do they live? Do they float on the water and swim up and down the pond or river all the time? Do they go on land? How do they move on land? In which three ways can water birds such as ducks move? How many ways can you move by yourself and with using machines?

What do I need?

Ask children what they need for themselves everyday, like food, clothes, air, water, shelter and warmth.

How do other animals the children know, e.g. a pet, get the same things?

Make a poster of what is needed and how the children obtain these things. Cut out pictures from magazines and so on of, for example, different foods, shops, crops, clothes and homes. You may be able to finds adverts for pet care and talk about those too.

Make photo journals of pet care and the children meeting some of their own needs.

What animals need

Ask older children to choose a well-known animal and find the answer for that species. Then choose another different animal. Find out the specific needs for that animal. Talk about how these animals are the same and how they are different to each other and the children. Suggested animals are: cats, dogs, chickens, garden birds e.g. blackbird, magpie or thrush, gerbils or hamsters, butterflies, mealworm beetle, stick insect, snail, ant, pigeon and squirrel.

Try filling in a table with them (see opposite). Cut out pictures or take your own and help the children to make a photo journal of things they need and where they get these things from.

Grouping wild animals

If you have models of zoo and farm animals, can the children group them? Are they mammals, birds or reptiles? What causes the children to allocate each model to the group they say it belongs to? What characteristics that they can see do they use to allocate the animals? Usually it is shape, number of legs and body covering.

Child's needs	How needs are met	Animal 1's needs	How needs are met	Animal 2's needs	How needs are met
Body covering to keep warm or cool	Clothes				
Food	Meat, fruits, vegetables				
Obtaining food?	Buy in shops, may grow fruits and vegetables				
Drink – all need water	Water, milk, fizzy drinks, tea				
Obtaining drink?	Water from tap, buy in shops				
How gets rid of waste fluid and food?	Uses a lavatory				
How gets oxygen?	Breathe in air				
Where lives: land, water, air?	On land				
What sort of shelter?	House				
Moves around how?	On legs, car, bicycle, scooter				
What dangers?	Traffic				
How long sleeps per 24 hrs?	8/10 hrs				
Lives with others?	Grown ups and brother sisters				

Fur and hair

If possible show the children a piece of fur (it can be synthetic), a piece of hair and some wool (sheepskin linings to gloves or boots can be used and some handbags also have a panel of animal skin or hair). Feel the skins; feel their own skin, which also has a covering of fine hair as do the different mammals. What do the hair coverings feel like?

Other covers

Look at pictures of other animals such as a hedgehog or a turtle. What body covering does a hedgehog have? The prickles are modified hairs.

What animals do children see at home?

What group do they belong to – mammals, birds, reptiles, amphibians, invertebrates such as insects or molluscs? How are these animals looked after? Why do they need to be looked after? Where do they live in the children's houses? Where would they live if they were not pets?

Everyday animals

What animals do the children see every day at school? On the way to school? At home? Other special places they visit? Where do children expect to see these animals? Can they see them all year round? If not, why not?

Where would children expect to see the following: greenflies, horses, sheep, snakes, blue bottles, butterflies, beetles, woodlice, slugs, snails, earthworms, frogs, bees, cats, pigeons, squirrels, cats, cows, ducks, fish, elephants.

Animals and offspring – mummies, daddies and babies

Are all baby animals just like their parents as soon as they are born?

Are you just like your parents now? Are babies? What is different?

What is a baby cat called? Is it like its mother? In what way is it the same? In what way is it different? Is the baby looked after when it is born?

What is a baby dog called? Is it like its mother? In what way is it the same? In what way is it different? Is the baby looked after when it is born?

What is a baby chicken called? Is it like its mother? In what way is it the same? In what way is it different? Is the baby looked after when it is born?

What is a baby blue bottle fly called? Is it like its mother? In what way is it the same? In what way is it different? Is the baby looked after when it is born?

What is a baby butterfly called? Is it like its mother? In what way is it the same? In what way is it different? Is the baby looked after when it is born?

What is a baby frog called? Is it like its mother? In what way is it the same? In what way is it different? Is the baby looked after when it is born?

What is a baby sheep called? Is it like its mother? In what way is it the same? In what way is it different? Is the baby looked after when it is born?

Same kind – different life stage

Find pictures or models of adult animals and their babies. Can the children match the babies to the parents? Can they give the names of the different animals?

Examples:

- Ram, nanny, kid – all goats
- Ram, ewe, lamb – all sheep
- Bull, cow, calf – all cattle
- Cockerel, hen, chick – all chickens
- Stallion, mare, foal – all horses
- Butterflies, chrysalis/pupa, caterpillar – all butterflies
- Frog, froglet, tadpole – all frogs
- Flies, pupa, maggot – all flies.

Can the children find pictures to illustrate these different kinds of the same animal?

 ## Moving animals

Try to find a snail and put it in a tray with some soil and some food (lettuce, for instance) and watch.

How does it move? If you have any water snails in an aquarium or can entice a land snail onto a piece of strong, see-through plastic sheeting and then look up at the snail so you see its underside you can usually see its mouth and the rippling of the muscular foot.

Make sure the snail is returned to where it was found.

Woodlice

Woodlice can be observed too but care must be taken to keep them moist. If you put them in a tray with wet food, e.g. a damp lettuce leaf at one end, they usually move to that. If you cover one end of the tray so it is dark woodlice usually choose that end. Put the same amount of food at the lighter end to make it a fair test!

Mealworms, an ideal class animal

Mealworm beetles living in a covered container or plastic aquarium are excellent classroom animals to use in order to observe the life history of an arthropod, larvae–pupa–adult, as well as to see how beetles and larva move.

Outcomes

After being involved in the above activities, which are only a few of many that can be undertaken that explore the variety of animal life, children should have developed a basic understanding of form, function and characteristic features that enable them to allocate a specimen to a group. They should be able to recognize the everyday local animals that they encounter.

6

Other living things – plants

Summary

Plants are green because they contain a pigment that enables them to capture the sun's energy to make food for their growth, and for animals that rely on plants to obtain their own energy. (Some animals eat other animals and obtain this energy secondhand.) Plants need light to grow properly. Plants are normally in one place fixed in the ground, with roots to anchor them. There are two main groups of plants: higher and lower. Lower plants were the first plants to evolve and reproduce. They are also non-vascular, which means they do not have the internal organs, the tubes called xylem and phloem, which carry food and water around the higher, vascular plants. Examples of these lower plants are mosses, lichens and ferns. These types of plants are also called cryptograms. Higher plants are either those with seeds or those that do not make seeds. Seed makers have flowers. Some plants have flowers and produce seeds in a fruit. Other plants make seeds but not flowers, while the lower plants make spores. Seeds are food stores for the baby plant to use in order to grow until it makes leaves to capture energy from the sun and in turn make its own.

> ## *Key words*
>
> Plant, photosynthesis, chlorophyll, vascular and non-vascular plants, roots, xylem, fibres, phloem, spores, alternation of generations, light, energy, monocotyledons, dicotyledons, anther, stamens, ovary, filaments, petals, sepals, leaves, weeds, evaporation, pollen grains, chromosomes, transpiration, cones, gymnosperms, angiosperms, prothallus, seeds.

Big ideas

Plants are green living organisms. They are green because they contain a chemical, chlorophyll, which enables them to use sunlight's energy to drive a chemical reaction called photosynthesis, which produces sugars. Chlorophyll is contained in the cells of plants, which have rigid cellulose walls, unlike animal cells. If a green plant is deprived of light it loses its green colour and turns yellowish white. Plants that still grow without light become long and straggly and lose their green colour.

Plants need more than just sunlight!

Apart from sunlight to drive the process of photosynthesis, plants also need elements such as magnesium and potassium. These they obtain from the soil through their roots. Hence, the other big difference (other than being green) between plants and animals, is that plants stay still where they grow unlike animals that move searching for food (with few exceptions).

Plants are more than just flowers

Although most children think of 'plants' as the name for flowers, in a similar way to how people generally think of the word 'animal' as synonymous with mammals, plants in fact have a number of distinct groups, including (in everyday language) flowers, fruits, vegetables, weeds, trees, herbs, bushes, grasses, vines, ferns, mosses, fungi and seaweeds. Fungi and the red seaweeds (red algae) are not considered 'plants' by botanists. The everyday grouping of 'plants' is usually assumed to mean flowers. Trees, bushes, fruits, vegetables and weeds are not regarded as flowers by non-scientists. Weeds are considered plants that grow in places where humans do not want them to. These are not botanical groups but an everyday human utilitarian one that children hear. There are more than 300,000 different kinds of plants and about two-thirds of them have seeds.

Two main plant groups

Biologically there are two main groups of plants: a smaller one of non-vascular plants (also called lower plants), and the large group of vascular plants (also called higher plants).

Higher plants

The higher plants have special tissues or organs for carrying water, minerals and photo-synthetic products through the plant. Each plant also has a root, stem and leaves, which contain these tubes. Many vascular plants also have strengthening fibres, some of which are used by humans to make items. Fibres can be seen in celery. The grit in pears is round fibres. Water contains minerals from the soil, which are in solution in the water and carried upwards in the plant in the xylem vessels while the food products from the leaves are carried downwards, away from the leaves, in the phloem tubes. The water is carried up through a process known as transpiration and as water evaporates from leaves it draws more water up the cells. Plants wilt if they do not have water to keep their cells full or turgid.

Seed makers, non-seed makers and spore makers

The higher plant group includes a number of groups. The largest is made up of the seed bearing plants (angiosperms or flowering plants) and gymnosperms (non-flowering seed producing plants, usually conifers), but also less developed plants such as club mosses, equisetum (horsetails) and ferns. These kinds of plants were around with the dinosaurs.

Different flowers, different shapes

Flowers do not look alike. Different groups have distinctive flower shapes but all contain the same parts. Daffodils and narcissi, usually yellow shading to white or orange, have petals surrounding a trumpet-shaped middle part in which the sex organs are kept. Some flowers are star-shaped, some are bell-shaped (such as blue bells), some are larger circles with yellow middles (such as buttercups) while some are two lipped (such as snap dragons or white dead nettle). Some kinds of plants, including clovers and chives, have many little flowers all held on one tight head. Some flowers, members of the pea family, have five petals, two of which look like wings at the side, a large one like a hood and two petals below the wings like a keel. Some tiny flowers are held on small stems to form a level platform of all these flowers, for example cow parsley. Some of these differently-shaped flowers may be seen on lawns, in gardens or on grass verges.

Compound flowers – many florets in one flower head

The flowers of the daisy and dandelion group of plants are called composite, and are actually made of two kinds of tiny flowers. The ray florets, which are large around the edge of the flowers, surround the middle of the flower with disc florets. A daisy shows this arrangement clearly. The white petals of a daisy are around the yellow disc florets in the middle. Dandelion and coltsfoot flowers only have the ray florets. The thistle family are spiny plants and have tight heads of purple colour from the disk florets. The ray florets are very, very small.

Seed making – the job of flowers

The role of flowers is to make seeds. They are the sex organs of the flowering plants.

Dicotyledonous plants' flowers have green sepals (usually) on the outside that cover the flower in bud, then the petals with definite numbers and shapes according to the kind of plant and the family to which it belongs. For example, pea flowers belong to the group that produce fruits as legumes, like pea pods, and have a bilaterally symmetrical flower as seen in the sweet pea or kidney bean plant, whereas the buttercup group has six petals arranged in a circle. Flowers have distinct petal colours; buttercups are usually yellow, for example. Yellow flowers tend to appear along with white ones as with snowdrops in the spring followed by flowers with other colours.

Seed makers but no flowers

The plants that produce seeds are divided into those that produce flowers and those that do not. The latter are the gymnosperms, which have seeds in cones with the seeds between the leaves; this can be easily seen in pinecones. Trees are flowering plants. They mostly lose their leaves in the winter and are called deciduous, with a few exceptions in some flowering trees such as holly. The non-flowering gymnosperms are non-deciduous and keep their leaves through the winter.

Flowering plants

The flowering plants are called the angiosperms; these are divided into the monocotyledons and the dicotyledons. A cotyledon is the seed leaf inside the seed. Dicotyledons have two, as in a bean or pea and monocotyledons only have one, as in a sweet corn fruit. Dicotyledonous plants have branched veins in their leaves, as seen in a rose leaf, whereas monocotyledons have parallel lines on their leaves, which tend to be long and thin, like those of daffodils or grass plants. The flowering plants are divided again into six subgroups called super orders, which are divided into orders, then smaller groups called families. Monocotyledons plants are classified into four super orders. The lily group and grasses group are common ones that most people have seen. If eaten, plants are more difficult to digest than animals and contain less energy and protein.

Reproductive parts – sex organs of flowers

The sex organs of flowering plants are in the middle of the flower. The stamens have two parts: the anther is at the top part and contains the pollen. The stalks on which the anther rests are called the filament. The female part of a flower is the stigma, which connects to the style and leads to the ovary where the female sex cells are found. The ovary develops into the fruit. The style is clearly seen in lilies and tulips. A pollen grain that

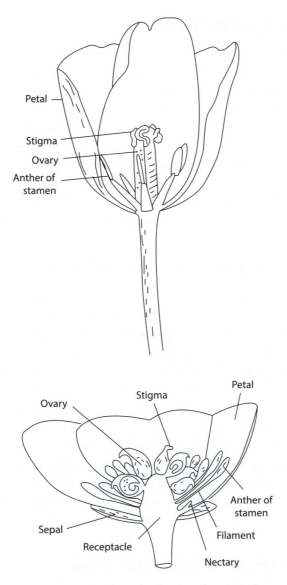

6.1 The reproductive parts (sex organs) of two kinds of seed making flowers. The top drawing is of a half-flower of a tulip, which has one seed leaf (monocotyledon) and the lower drawing is of a buttercup, which has two seed leaves (dicotyledons). The male reproductive organs are the stamens, made up of an anther to which the male sex cells (pollen grains) are attached and a stalk, the filament. The female's organs are in the middle of the flower. The stigma is where the pollen grains land, while the seed is in the ovary.

lands on the style of another flower grows a tube down to the ovary, through which the male nucleus moves so it can fertilize the female sex cell. When people give flowers they are actually giving the sex organs of another living thing.

Separate sexes, separate flowers

Some flowering plants have the male parts and female parts in separate flowers. Sometimes, as in holly trees, the male and female flowers are on different plants. Catkins of hazel, birch and willow trees show this. The catkins are long and dangly so the pollen grains are caught by the wind and blown onto the smaller female flowers. Flowers that do not use wind have different ways to ensure their pollen carried to another flower. Some flowers have perfume such as honeysuckle, which attracts animals that carry their pollen to another; these are animals with long tongues such as moths that can reach right into the flower. Others, such as Jack in the pulpit, wild arum or lords and ladies, exude a smell of rotting meat, which attracts certain flies. Honeybees visit flowers to collect pollen and yellow sacs of this may be seen on the back legs of bees.

Spore makers and alternation of generations

Ferns have two different kinds of tubes inside their stems and roots called xylem and phloem. They have stems, leaves and roots so are therefore grouped with vascular plants; however, they reproduce by spores not seeds and thus do not have flowers. There are also two distinct generations in plants in their reproductive life. The higher plant form like a tree or rose bush (called the generation form) is, as in humans, made up of cells with the full set of chromosomes. Chromosome numbers are halved to make sex cells in all organisms and this stage of the plant (as in humans and other animals) happens in special reproductive organs. Each sex cell has half the number of chromosomes of the plant so that when these sex cells meet, their product has the full set of chromosomes again (just as happens in sexual reproduction in animals). Mosses also have this alternation of generation. One generation that makes the spores is what we usually see. This grows on a small flat body called a prothallus, which makes up the other generation.

Lower plant anatomy – non vascular plants

The lower plants, for example the non-vascular mosses, are smaller and do not have any specialized tubes, xylem and phloem and no roots, stems or leaves. The principal generation phase in non-vascular plants is usually the gametophyte, which is haploid with one set of chromosomes per cell. In these plants, generally only the spore stalk and capsule are diploid, which means they have two sets of each chromosome. In ferns the spores, which will grow into a new plant, are in capsules on the back of their fronds, the leaf-like structures.

The two main groups that children are likely to see are mosses and liverworts. Scientifically these groups are called bryophytes. Mosses are small green plants found on trees, in lawns and on the ground, particularly in damp places such as at the foot of the walls of buildings. Mosses with their fruiting capsules are very distinctive. Mosses and liverworts do not have tubes to carry water like the higher plants, they have to absorb water through their cells and this limits their size. The mosses children are likely to see have distinct spore capsules on stalks coming from the small green plant.

Green algae – seaweeds and pondweed

Another group of plants children may see are green algae, which live in water and photosynthesize. Some ponds are full of green strands of algae called blanket weed. Lettuce and other green plants in seawater water belong to this group. Red algae are not considered plants any more; neither are fungi that have a very different structure and do not make their own food, hence are not green. They are discussed in Chapter 7.

How long do plants live?

Herbaceous plants that grow in a year then die after they have produced their fruit and then seeds are called annual plants. Others that live two years are called biannual while those that live a long time and reappear every year, such as a rose bush, lavender bush or clump of Michaelmas daisies, are called perennials. Trees and other plants that take a number of years to grow from the seed to the adult plant are also perennials. Gardeners sow annuals every year and the bedding plants that appear in gardens and window boxes in summer are mostly annuals. A grass plant is perennial. Seeds are dry when released from the fruit and, before they will develop, need to take in water. Shoots and stems grow upwards against the gravitational pull of the earth whereas roots always grow downwards. When the seed leaves (cotyledons) and shoots emerge they are not green but once in the light they develop their green colour. If light is cut off from a stem and leaves those parts of the plant lose their green colour. The green reappears when the light once again reaches these parts.

Human food – fruits, seeds, stems and leaves

Seeds are contained in fruits. Humans and other animals eat these fruits. Some of what we call vegetables are also fruits containing seeds. Tomatoes and cucumbers have seeds inside so are real fruits, whereas other parts of plants that humans call vegetables, such as cauliflower and broccoli, are the flowers of the plant. Celery is a stem of that kind of plant while lettuce and cabbages are the leaves. Potatoes are the swollen underground stems of plants. Peas and beans are the seeds. Apples, oranges and bananas are the fruit with the seeds inside. A white rice grain is the seed from rice with its husk or fruit removed. Rice plants are a kind of cereal derived from grasses. Sweet corn is the fruit of a type of corn and the seed is inside the kernel.

Talking and doing

The objectives of the following actives are to help children understand that plants are green and that not all plants produce flowers. We humans and other animals eat parts of plants and the animal world depends on them. Through looking at specimens, including fruits, seeds and what we call vegetables and fruits, children should be able to recognize the parts of plants and their job in the life of the plant as well as the parts of higher plants. Young children like colours and shapes so can learn to recognize a variety of everyday flowers, learning their names and the names of their parts. Talking about plants in the lives of children and learning the appropriate everyday words is an important part of this set of activities.

What is green?

Look outside and ask children what things that they see are green; for example, lamp posts, street signs, front doors, cars or people's clothes.

Which of the green things are plants? Point them out to children. Give them the names of the plants. Give a superordinate group name, such as tree, and a specific name, such as apple tree, pine tree, rose bush or daisy plant.

Explain that some plants have flowers, and that trees and bushes have flowers too and make seeds. Conifers, trees with needle-shaped leaves, do not have flowers but still make seeds.

Talk about a leaf

Collect some leaves, starting with the same kind if possible. The leaves can be from a deciduous tree (broadleaved), from a conifer or from a herbaceous plant such as a house plant.

Hold up the leaf and ask the children to describe it in terms of shape, size, colour, thickness and anything else you can think of. Hold up a small piece of white paper, or coloured paper, and ask the children to describe the piece of paper. What are the similarities between the leaf and the paper, and what are the differences?

Below ground

Grow a seed such as a pea, some rape or cress in a see-through container so that the children can see and comment upon the shoot above soil and the root below the ground.

Parts of a plant

If possible, pull up a weed in the garden. What part of the plant was above the ground? What was below?

Ask what parts of the plant they can see above the ground, and then when a plant is uprooted (or the seedling placed on a piece of paper so you can look at it); where is each part (root, stem, leaves)?

Lawns

Many children think that the word 'grass' is synonymous with lawn, not realizing that a lawn is made up of many small grass plants. Examine a lawn and let the children work out that it is not one big green plant but many little plants together.

If you can find a grass plant that has not been mown down but has developed its flowers on a long stem, show that to the children. They usually do not understand that grass plants have flowers too and produce pollen (a fact known to many hay fever sufferers).

Plant safari

Make a safari – an expeditionary walk around the setting or school. Have the children make a plant spying tube from a kitchen towel roll. They can point their plant spy tube at different parts of the ground that they can see. Have they seen a plant? Is it a plant? Why? Do they know its name?

A plant safari with a camera is an ideal opportunity to record what is growing around school. If it is made several times a year at the beginning and end of each term, you can all talk about the pictures and point out what has changed and what has remained the same. Usually, for example, the trees will be there all the time but they may look different in spring, summer, autumn and winter, whereas evergreen trees will be the same. Why? What about the bedding plants or bulbs such as crocuses and daffodils? Are there daisy flowers in the grass during winter?

Flower shapes

If children know the basic shapes – star, circle, oblong and bell (like an oval with a flat bottom) – they may be able to recognize the shapes in flowers. What different shapes of flowers can the children see around outside or in the pot plants inside? This is again an opportunity for a photo journal or for the cutting out of pictures from catalogues when such a plant shape has been sighted.

Make a chart of flower shapes and colours:

Shape	Name of flowers	Colours	Where found
Circle			
Star			
Two lipped			
Cup shaped			

Conifer

Christmas trees are evergreens and do not lose their leaves in the winter. The leaves are needle shaped, like other pine trees.

Look at these needle-shaped leaves and compare them with the shape of leaves from a deciduous tree that are flatter and usually much softer. Try a silver birch, privet or apple leaf.

Prickles

Look at holly tree leaves; they are shiny to cut down water loss and the leaves do not fall off in winter. The leaf edge has sharp points, which prickle. Thistles have prickles, as do blackberries on their stems.

Pinecone

If you can find some pinecones show the children the parts of the cone and the scales between which are the seeds. They are winged seeds. Other conifers also produce different sorts of cones. Look on cypresses or cedar trees that are often in gardens as hedges or specimen trees.

Leaves

How many different shapes of leaf can the children find? If there are many trees and bushes, collect an assortment. Ask the children to sort them into similar shapes. What shapes are found? Many leaves are long and straight, like very elongated oblongs, with a point at the end; for example, grass and daffodils. These leaves have two shapes, the long rectangle and the small triangle at the tip. Some, like lily of the valley, are long ovals with a tip. Some leaves are compound leaves such as horse chestnuts made up of a number of leaves that are all the same shape. They all form this compound leaf.

Are there any square leaves? Any round ones? Any triangular leaves or do any leaves have these shapes incorporated into them?

Lines and branches: grouping plants – monocotyledons and dicotyledons

Which leaves have lines running up them and which have one mid line and lines that branch off? Look at everyday plants you can see or photos from plant magazines or the Internet. Can the children say which plants are monocotyledons and which are dicotyledons from observing for themselves?

Make a collection of leaves and ask the children to sort them into lined and branched. Monocotyledon plants such as grass have parallel lines on their leaves, whereas dicotyledon plants such as pelargonium (mistakenly called geraniums by many people), daisies and roses have branched lines or veins often with a mid rib with side branches. Ask the children to say why they have allocated the leaf to that particular group.

Matching shapes with leaves

Try cutting out small shapes and have the children try fitting the shapes over leaves. Small and large plastic counters can be used as templates. Small geometric plastic shapes can be placed over leaves. Children enjoy tracing round these shapes first, and their tracings can then be cut out for their own leaf shape search.

Are leaves green when it is dark?

How would children investigate what happens to green plants at night when there is no sun? Do they lose their green? What ideas do the children have?

 ## Trees

Use outline drawings or photographs of different trees so that you can see the outline of the branches with leaves on or look at the trees that can be seen from school or home.

Have shapes such as oval, triangle, thin rectangle and circle, for example that the children can hold up in front of themselves between them and the tree. What shapes are the trees?

Make a list, draw the trees and make a photo journal of trees seen:

- Tree 1 (name if known) is like a _____ shape.
- Tree 2 (name if known) is like a _____ shape.
- Tree 3 (name if known) is like a _____ shape.
- I like the _____ shaped tree best because . . .

Flowers on trees

In the spring and summer, have the children look at trees around them, at pictures from the Internet or in magazines of trees in flower. What local trees have flowers? Where are the flowers? This is an ideal photo journal opportunity! How long do the flowers last?

Fruits

Look at pictures of trees or trees around in autumn in the northern hemisphere. This is after the trees have had their flowers. Can you see any fruits? Where are they? What has happened to the flowers? When do the plants have fruits? All year or at special times?

Some fruits on trees are very distinct. Look out for them: fruits such as acorns; conkers in their spiky case (the conker is the seed); beech mast, where the cases are prickly and the fruit the beechnut inside; cherries and apple, which are fleshy fruits with the seeds inside. The red holly berries or those of hawthorn or rowan trees are the fruits.

Obtain some apples and look at them; see the remains of the flower at the top of the apple, the opposite end from the stalk. Cut an apple open and see the seeds in the middle in special compartments.

Leaving home – fruit dispersal

Fruits contain seeds. Seeds need to leave the parent and move away so that they can grow into new plants. The fleshy fruits attract animals that eat them, and the seeds pass through their gut and are deposited with the waste food of the animal somewhere else.

Some fruits drop to the ground, such as apples, but others such as sycamore winged fruits or lime tree or ash tree 'helicopters' are blown by the wind.

Some flowering plants have wind mechanisms for distributing their fruits with their seeds, as in the case of dandelion clocks or the seeds of willow, which look fluffy and cover everything on which they land with a white layer because there are so many.

Root stem or leaf to fruit?

How can you tell which is which? Have a collection of fruit and vegetables. You can start with the plastic models from the early years resources, e.g. plastic bananas. Help the children to name the different fruits and vegetables and talk about where they have seen them, what we humans do with them and from where we obtain them.

Look at fruits and vegetables. Which of the plant parts are stem? Examples of stems we eat are celery and potatoes (underground stem). Watercress shows stems and leaves and occasionally you can even see small flowers.

Which are leaves? These include lettuce and cabbages. Onions are the swollen bases of leaves.

Roots come from the ground, such as carrots, radishes, parsnips, beetroot, swedes and turnips. If you cut through a radish, parsnip or carrot you will see the vascular bundle in the centre of the root. In a stem the vascular bundles are small and arranged in a circle towards the edge of the stem, for example in a cross section of the base of a celery stem. Cut open round ones, such as a courgette (also called zucchini or summer squash) or marrow, turnip, tomatoes. Those that show seeds inside them, like courgettes and tomatoes, are fruits.

More fruits

Have some real apples and oranges, a banana, grapes (not seedless) as well as tomatoes.

What part of the plant are these items?

If they are fruits, what must they have inside them? The answer is seeds. Cut them open and see.

Swollen stems

Where are the eyes?

Have some potatoes (not new ones, where the eyes are more difficult to see). Look at the potatoes and find the eyes. These are buds on these swollen underground stems. Roots do not have buds.

Growing in the dark

If potatoes are kept very long they will start growing stems as white shoots from the eyes (the buds). Ask the children what they think would happen if you put the potatoes in a box (shoe box or cereal packet) in the dark and left them. Bring in a potato that has been left in a vegetable cupboard or rack and show children what happens after a few weeks. What colour are these stems? What happens if they are left in the dark? What happens if they are left in sunlight? Try leaving the potatoes and see what happens. Were the children accurate in their prediction?

Potato magic

Put an old potato in a box with a small hole at one end to let in light. Ask the children what they think will happen (already knowing that potatoes have eyes that will grow stems). Leave the box for some time and watch. Open the box quickly each day and draw or photograph what is seen. Usually the potatoes grow a stem, which grows towards the light.

No light

Find a patch of grass plants. Look at the plants. What colour are they?

Cover a small patch with a stone or piece of wood so that no light can get reach the plants. Go back a week later. What has happened to the plants that had no light? What colour are they?

In the dark

Obtain two green plants, perhaps grow beans from seed. Put one in the dark and leave one in the light making sure they are watered in their pots first.

After a few days, what is happening to the plant in the dark? Crowns of the vegetable broccoli (really the flowers) go yellow if left in cupboard without light for several days.

Seeds

What kind of seeds have the children seen?

Bring in a collection and ask the children to sort them into groups – whatever way they want. What are their criteria for the sorting?

Have some small seeds such as onion, which are black, sunflower seeds, pumpkin seeds, mung beans, peas, and broad beans, nasturtium. How do children sort them? What are their reasons? Colour? Size? Shapes? Smooth or bumpy? How many different ways of sorting seeds can they find? Weighing? Measuring? Sieving?

Packet seeds

What do they notice about the seeds if they came from packets compared with seeds from the plant? What happens to fleshy fresh seeds, e.g. nasturtiums, if they are left a long time? Try fresh peas and broad beans.

Growing seeds

What has to happen to the seed before it will grow?

Take 20 dry peas. What do they look like? Feel like? Keep ten in a dish. Soak the other ten in another dish with cold water overnight.

What is different the next day when you compare them with the unsoaked peas?

Growing

Which do the children think will grow? Why?

Plant non-soaked and soaked peas in plastic cups so you can all look through and see the seeds. Keep the seeds in place with a piece of kitchen towel folded and placed in the cup.

Watch! What happens? Does anything appear? This seed watch is ideal for a photo journal or a 'Seed Watch' folder.

Up or down?

Of the seeds that grow what part of the plant has appeared first? What part is second? Which direction do they grow?

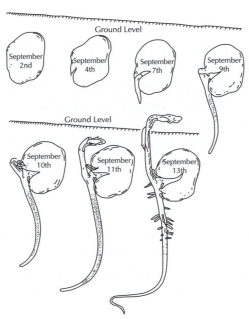

6.2 Seeds do not develop overnight; first they must be soaked to absorb water. The seed labeled September 2nd is such a seed. The shoot only appears above ground 11 days later. The root is the first part of the plant to emerge, followed a few days later by the shoot, which pushed up through the soil towards the light. If you 'plant' the seeds in a see-through jar with kitchen towel to support them the seed still develops in the same sequence.

Soak broad bean seeds or peas again and then repeat the planting. Put each seed inside a plastic cup between the wall of the cup and kitchen towel or newspaper screwed up in the middle of the cup. The paper is there to keep the seeds pressed against the side of the cup. Put some seeds in upside down, some sideways, some with the root pocket pointing down. This is the pointed yellow part on the pea.

Sideways seeds

What happens to the root on the seeds planted sideways and upside down? What happens to the shoot? One grows to the ground; the other, the shoot, to the air. What happens to the root and shoot in the sideways bean?

Inside a seed

What is inside the seed? The answer is the baby plant and food that its mother put there. The food is what we eat, the fleshy part of the bean or pea, and the baby plant is the very small white or yellow bit. If you look inside a pea or bean pod with its seed still in you can see the stalk that attaches the seed to its mother, just like the umbilical cord of a mammal that attaches the baby to the placenta.

Baby sweet corn

Put a single sweet corn fruit from a tin of sweet corn on a flat surface on some paper towel. If the fluid comes out too, dry the seeds. It is easiest to pour out a few fruits from the tin into a saucer and then pick them out and place on the towel or something else and then the children can look. Ask the children to find the white part, at the flat end of the yellow part. If they press just behind this towards the other end, the embryo should pop out. The children can see the embryo and the single food store of the monocotyledon plants.

Flowers

Lilies have amazing stamens with large anther covered with dark golden pollen (these contain the male sex cells). Show the children the stamens on lilies. Can they find them on other flowers? Tulips have prominent stamens too as well as a very distinct style in the middle. Roses have many rings of yellow stamens, and daffodil stamens are also easily seen.

[If lily pollen gets on anyone's clothes if you are looking at real lilies, it comes off if you place a piece of sellotape over it, sticky side down, and pull.]

How many flower colours?

How many different colours can the children see in flowering plants around you? Make a list of how many different coloured petals have been seen.

Dangly flowers

Find the catkin-bearing trees around school and have a catkin walk where these special flowers can be seen in the spring. If this is not possible, find images on the Internet and show the children. Ask them if they have ever seen any in real life.

Ferns

Find a fern plant to observe. If there are none locally a plant can be bought at a garden centre. These types of plants are usually called *Dryopteris*, and will feature fronds (the name for what looks like leaves) with a central 'stem' off which come green 'leaves'. Look on the back of the fronds and you may see brown dots, which are the spore containers.

What colour are ferns? Have the ferns any flowers? Where do ferns grow? Have children seen them in gardens or parks? Where else may they have seen them?

Mosses

Ask children to go on a moss search and note where the mosses grow. Are they in the middle of the playground? Do they live where it is very dry? Do they grow in wetter areas? In the spring, bowls of bulbs are sold in florists and supermarkets with moss covering the bulb fibre.

Picture wall

Find pictures of mosses and ferns. You may have plant catalogues featuring ferns and be able to find pictures in the Internet. Paste them to a piece of card or stick them on a board. Ask children to talk about the pictures. Give them the names, and tell them which is a fern and which is a moss.

Water and flowers

Water and plants – wilting

You need a few cut flowers in a container with water to make the observations in this investigation. Plants need water to keep them upright unless, like trees, they are woody.

Look at some plants growing. Are they upright? Look at flowers in a vase. Are the flowers standing upright? What happens if cut flowers are just left on a table?

Watering the garden

Ask the children if they have seen plants in gardens. Where in the garden have they seen them? Find some photographs of hanging baskets and patio tubs from gardening magazines. Put then them on the table or a wall. Talk about them and give the children the names of the containers. Ask if they have seen anyone water the plants in the flower beds or baskets or tubs. Ask if they know why grown ups water plants.

Have they seen plants in hanging baskets? What do grown ups use to water the plants? Obtain a watering can or pictures of them. Talk about how they are used. Let children practise watering a plant with a watering can. Many learning areas have small watering cans, which are much easier for them to handle.

Why do gardeners water their gardens when there has been little rain? What happens to hanging baskets and to plants if they do not have water?

Why do we put cut flowers in water?

Obtain two similar cut flowers with soft stems (like two daisies) and place one in a small pot of water and the other in an identical pot but with no water. What happens? The same investigation can be done with sticks (stems) of celery too. Without water the cut part of the plant loses its firmness and becomes floppy.

Outcomes

After investigating some of the activities in this section and looking at the plants they can see around, talking about them and naming both them and their parts, these young botanists should have a fundamental understanding of the nature of the concept 'plant' as well as the vocabulary with which to talk about them. They should know that plants are very important and there are many more varieties than just the flowering plants. They may also learn that fruits containing seeds are made by flowering plants and the seeds grow into new plants; the children should grasp that humans and other animals eat many of these as well as other parts of plants.

7

Other living things – fungi, bacteria and algae

Summary

There are other groups of living things besides plants and animals. Fungi, bacteria and algae are the main ones. Scientists consider there to be five kingdoms of living things. Many such organisms can live without oxygen and are called anaerobic. Fungi live off other living things and take their food, but also break down former living things and absorb the chemicals in them. This process is termed decomposing. Disease-causing bacteria are spread by human activity, particularly by contaminated hands; hence, hand washing is a vital habit to learn. Some fungi and algae live together to form lichens. Other fungi are used in food making as well as in drug production, e.g. penicillin, to fight bacteria that cause infection. Such drugs are called antibiotics.

> ### Key words
>
> Anaerobic, monera, bacteria, algae, archebacteria, eubacteria, protozoa, photosynthesis, chloroplasts, sponges, multicellular, eukaryotic cell, substrate, fungi, decomposers, kingdoms, spores, gills, cap, mycorrhiza, protista, indicators, disease, drugs, resistance, symbiosis, parasites, food manufacture, yoghurts, cheeses, yeasts, disease spread, antibiotics.

 Big ideas

Five kingdoms of living things

While the different kinds of plants and animals are familiar to most people there are other kingdoms of living things. The number of kingdoms varies, but the present view is that there are five. The five are animals, plants, fungi, protista and monera. The members of each kingdom must meet a number of criteria in order to be included, taking into consideration their anatomy and how they obtain food.

Viruses

Viruses are not considered as part of these kingdoms. The monera is the name given to the smallest of these simple organisms. Their nucleus containing their genetic materials is not inside a membrane. Monera either absorb their food or they can use the energy of the sun through photosynthesis. Examples are blue and green algae and a range of bacteria such as E. coli.

Viruses are minute and cause a huge amount of disease across all organisms. Antibiotics do not affect viruses. They do however kill many bacteria although, if over used, bacteria can develop into forms that are resistant to the antibiotics, which will no longer have an effect.

Bacteria are everywhere and very small, hence being called microbes. When a baby is born it normally obtains bacteria from the secretions of its mother as it descends the birth canal. New babies need bacteria to develop immunity against other disease-causing organisms. Babies delivered by caesarean section do not receive much of this natural introduction to bacteria. Recent research shows that all babies obtain some essential bacteria from their mother whilst in the uterus. Some bacteria cause disease in humans such diphtheria, tonsillitis and food poisoning. Other bacteria are needed in the human (and other organisms) to help them work efficiently, such as some kinds of bacteria found in the digestive system.

Two divisions of bacteria?

Some biologists consider that bacteria, none of which has a nucleus, should be divided into two groups; one group called true bacteria (eubacteria), and another containing bacteria-like organisms that live in very specialized habitats with no oxygen, called archea. Living without oxygen is termed anaerobic; our muscles work without oxygen for a short time when we use them a lot, such as when running. Afterwards, we breathe deeply and our muscles hurt as the body 'pays off the oxygen debt', making up for working without oxygen. Anaerobic living things exist in places such as the deep oceanic vents on the sea floor or in hot springs.

Spread of disease by bacteria and viruses

Many diseases are spread by touch so it is very important to keep hands clean, especially after using lavatories. E. coli bacteria live in humans usually without any effect, but if ingested can cause illness. A human sneeze contains millions of viruses so it is important to catch the cloud of a sneeze in a tissue that is then thrown away and to wash hands afterwards. It is just as important not to cough over people as the water spray that comes from the mouth also contains disease-causing organisms if the cougher has an infection.

Bacteria helpful to humans

Some human foods are made with the help of bacteria. Yoghurt is an easily available food. It is made from fermented milks, which contain bacteria *(lactobacilli)* that produce the lactic acid from a sugar in milk called lactose, through anaerobic (without oxygen) preparation. After a few days milk turns sour and this action is caused by bacteria producing an action-producing acid that makes milk coagulate, appear thicker and taste tart so most people don't like to drink it.

Humans fighting viruses and bacteria

Humans fight diseases themselves through their immune system. Our bodies recognize some disease-causing microorganisms that we have 'met' previously and can 'fight' them. This is the basis of immunizations, when dead or weakened bacteria or viruses are introduced into our bodies so that the body develops the strategies for fighting them off. Bacteria can change and become resistant to antibiotics. This can happen if antibiotics are used a lot. Unfortunately, some disease-causing organisms, particularly the influenza virus and the MRSA bacteria that causes a lot of the infections found in hospitals, can change their genetic make up quickly and become resistant to our immunity, meaning that the drugs that were used to destroy them are no longer effective. Many diseases are spread by touch, so it is important to keep washing hands. When infections are in the body, it reacts by becoming hotter in an attempt to kill the causative microbe by a temperature rise. This accounts for the raised temperature when we are ill with these sorts of infectious diseases.

Protista

The next largest group of living things is the protista, nearly all of which have a large single cell with a nucleus enclosed by a membrane. Such a cell is called eukaryotic and while many species are solitary some come together to form colonies, such as volvox. These organisms that take in food and absorb it through their surfaces are amoeba, paramecium. They may also use photosynthesis, in which case they have chloroplasts and look green, as shown by certain algae and protozoan. There are around 6,000 species of red algae, ranging in form from single-celled organisms to those that are made up of many cells. Red algae also contain a number of pigments beside chlorophyll, one of which reflects the red light in the spectrum hence causing the organisms to look red. Such red algae may be seen in rock pools and on coral reefs around the world, often called red seaweeds.

Fungi

Fungi are not plants but they are living things. They are not green and do not make their own food. They are made of filaments and have the eukaryotic cells, which are specialized. These organisms absorb food through their filaments. Familiar examples of members of the fungi kingdom are mushrooms, which we can buy in shops; bracket fungi, which may be found on trees; moulds such as those that appear on bread or other food left out and yeast. Fungi cause some infections of humans, such as thrush and poisoning.

Fungi contain no chlorophyll because they do not manufacture their food using the sun's energy, unlike plants. Their cell walls are made of chitin, not cellulose like a plant's. There are about 400 different kinds of fungi including mushrooms and toadstools as well as moulds, mildews and fungi called rusts. Most fungi obtain their nutrients from dead plants and animals. In fact, fungi are part of the important groups of organisms that break down living material to its components and are thus called decomposers. Some fungi are single-celled and called chytrids. It was a chytrid fungus that infected frogs worldwide and caused many to die.

Reproduction in fungi

Fungi can reproduce in several ways. A few fungi reproduce asexually but most reproduce sexually, by making spores. The structure of these reproductive or spore making parts is often used to group fungi. The spores have to be distributed and some fungi do this using explosive mechanisms or relying on an external force compressing them – puff balls seen on lawns do this. The 'puff' that is shot out contains a cloud of spores. Other fungi, such as mushrooms and toadstools, release spores from their gills situated under the cap.

Living off another – symbiosis

Some fungi have a symbiotic relationship with other organisms, obtaining their food from their host but also providing something for them in return; unlike a parasite, which just takes from its host, like tapeworms do from mammals. Mycorrhiza fungi often live with the roots of certain plants – such white strands can be seen round the roots of pine trees, for example.

Lichens – a partnership of fungus and algae

Lichens may be seen on trees and stones in non-polluted air. They are a combination of an algae and a fungus. The body of the lichen is formed by a fungus that encloses a kind of algae named photobionts. Photosynthesis by the algae in the lichen provides the

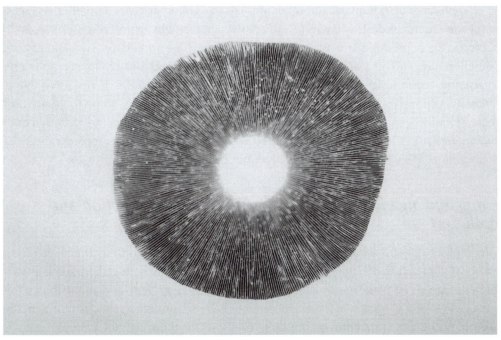

7.1 Spore prints of a fungus. A mushroom.

carbohydrates needed for this combination organism while the fungus obtains the minerals and water. Some animals such as the ant-like insects called termites in Africa grow fungus gardens in their termite mounds.

Fungi – harmful and helpful to humans

Many fungi cause disease to other organisms; ringworm and athletes foot are common examples. On the other hand, some fungi are very useful to humans. Yeasts are used in cooking, such as bakers' yeast in bread making, where the yeast's reaction produces the carbon dioxide that makes the dough rise. Yeast is crucial in the fermentation process to produce alcohol, which is used making drinks such as beer.

Fungi are used in making some human foods, particularly cheese. You can see the fungi if you look at blue cheeses. Camembert and Roquefort cheeses are made with two different types of penicillin fungi, as is Stilton. Fermenting soybeans with a type of fungus called *Aspergillus oryzae* produces soy sauce.

Animals that eat grass, such as cows, are called ruminants and have four chambered stomachs, each with a different function. The gut of cows contains bacteria, fungi and proteins, which can break down the cellulose and digests the grass, thus providing the animal with nutrients.

Some fungi help humans and other animals in fighting disease. Penicillin and other fungi were found to destroy bacteria and are used in the fight against diseases caused by bacteria. Such products are called antibiotics. The blue mould on some foods is a penicillin fungus. There are other fungi that are used as food for humans. Some people in autumn go on fungi forays to collect wild mushrooms, but this is not advisable as many are poisonous and it is better to buy mushrooms in a store. Some fungi are used recreationally because of the effect they have on humans. Fly Agaric, the toadstool often shown in pictures in fairy stories, bright red with white spots, is poisonous. It is found in areas with acid soils, associated with silver birch trees.

Fungi and algae work together – indicators of direction and pollution

Green algae may be seen as green patches on walls and the north-facing sides of tree trunks. Other kinds of algae, filamentous ones, form blanket weed in some ponds. Lichens appear in places with unpolluted air. Some logs, trees and other things (my canvas swinging garden seat for example) may have silvery-green shapes on them; this is probably lichen. Sometimes on buildings or elsewhere there are green circular patches or orange ones of lichens, the combinations of an algae and a fungus.

Animals and plants

The other kingdoms of living things are the animals and plants. Mosses, ferns, flowering and non-flowering plants are made up of many cells with the nucleus in a membrane and do not have their own locomotory mechanism. These living things obtain their food needs through photosynthesis. This is the process of capturing the energy of the sun and using it to combine chemicals to form sugars. These plants also use minerals, which they absorb from the substance in which they live, usually soil. The animal kingdom members are also multicellular, with the eukaryotic cell that in plants is specialized for many functions. Animals have to obtain their food ready made and take it into their bodies. The simplest are the sponges. The most complex are the primate group to which humans belong. The fungi are multicellular, but neither plant nor animal. Frequently people in everyday talk use the term mushroom for all fungi. True mushrooms are a specific kind of fungi.

Talking and doing

Working through these activities should assist young learners in consolidating their understanding of non-plants and animals including disease-causing bacteria and bacteria beneficial to other organisms, including humans. They should acquire the 'big idea' that plants make food and animals have to actively find their food ready made. However, some organisms live off others and take food from their host. On the other hand, some of these living things are helpful to humans, particularly in cooking or in making drugs to fight diseases caused by other living things.

Milk

Getting to know milk

Obtain a small mug, a small bowl and some milk.

What is milk? What makes ordinary milk? Where does it come from before it goes to the shops for us to buy? In what ways do humans use milk? How many different ways can the children think of?

Talk about milk

Explain that most of the milk that we use is from cows who produce milk for their babies, called calves. Sometimes people have goats' milk, made by female goats for their babies or kids, just as human mothers also produce milk for their babies.

Can milk change?

Show the children a small jug of fresh milk. What does the milk look like? Smell like? Does it pour easily? Leave it out for few days then look again. Has it changed? In what ways?

Can you slow down changes in milk?

What do the children think? Where did they learn their ideas?

Put a small amount of the fresh milk in a small container and keep it in the refrigerator. (Do children know what a refrigerator does?) Is the refrigerated milk the same as the milk left out in the room after the same time? If there is a difference, what can have caused it?

Washing hands

Dirty towels

Have some blocks of soap to wash hands, paper towels and cloth towels.

Why do we use soap to wash our hands? Ask children to notice what happens to their dirty hands if they just hold them under running water and then wipe them on a paper towel. What colour is the towel? What happens if they then wash their hands using soap to rub over their hands, rinse it off and then dry their hands? Does this method make the towel as dirty?

A soap alternative – spraying hands

What happens to a towel if you dry your hands on a towel after you use hand sprays?

Air or towel?

Ask children to say whether they think drying their hands with a towel is better at getting all the water off them than letting their hands dry in the air by waving them about. What do they think? Why do they think that?

Paper towel drying factor

Are paper towels as good as getting the water off the hands as fabric towels? What do the children think and why do they think that? Try it out. Make it a fair test by rubbing hands the same number of times whether they use a paper towel or fabric one.

Body temperature

Ask the children which parts of their body feel hottest, e.g. fingers, behind the ear, under the arm.

The nearer a part is to the core of the body the warmer it is (like under the arms or round your middle); the further away the cooler the part is (like tips of toes or fingers).

How can you keep the cool parts of your body warm when it is cold? What clothes can you wear?

Cooling down

How can you cool down when the air temperature is hot? What clothes do you wear then?

Mushrooms

Meet a mushroom

Bring some fresh mushrooms bought from a shop. Try to buy some button or baby mushrooms too as well as those with open caps where you can see the gills.

Ask the children what they are. How do they describe them? Colour, shape; what are the two main shapes? (Stalk and cap.)

Button and caps

What is the difference between a button mushroom and a big mushroom? Show each kind to the children. What do they observe? What do they say are the differences?

The button mushrooms are young ones and have no gills showing but a veil, a thin white membrane under the cap, and are much whiter. The older mushrooms show their gills on the underside of the cap. These gills are where the spore of the mushrooms are produced (see Figure 7.1).

Filaments

Pull or cut off the stalks of mushrooms and place them on a piece of white paper or a plate. With a sharp pencil or a toothpick see if you can see the strands that make the stalk; these are the filaments that make up the mushroom. They do not have any internal organs like plants do or fibres like in celery stalks.

Spore prints

Have a piece of glass, thick see-through plastic or some white paper and cut off the stalks of the mushrooms. Place them gill-side down on the paper or glass and leave them overnight. Cover the mushroom with a glass or see-through container to stop any air current blowing in and disturbing the spores that drop out of the gills of the mature mushroom. What do you see when you remove the caps? What shape is the pattern? What shapes make it up? Why are there white lines? Where does the dark colour come from? Ask the children what they think (see Figure 7.1).

Fungus walk

If you have grounds around school to visit take a walk, particularly in the autumn. Ask the children if they see any fungi growing. Look on old dead trees. Sometimes you see bracket fungi growing on the trunk of a tree. There may be some on a dead branch or trunk lying on the ground. You may see a bright orange fungus on dead damp twigs; this fungus appears as orange dots. Puff balls are sometimes seen on a lawn or flowerbed. An ink cap mushroom has a wide white base/stem with scales on it, and the base narrows at the top where there is a black cap.

Fairy rings

In the autumn many fungi appear to produce their spores. Sometimes on lawns you can see a ring of toadstools; this is often called a fairy ring.

Don't touch!

Don't touch any of the fungi that the children find but make a photo journal of 'Our fungus walk'.

Grow a fungus

Place a damp piece of bread that has been left out in the air for a while in a sealed see-through container. Ensure there are no holes.

Put the tub in a warm place and watch.

Soon you will see a mould appear; first a white strand, and then some fruiting bodies grow, that look like balls on top of a stalks. This is a fungus.

Keep covered

Ask children what they think would happen if you were to leave out foods that fungi may land and then grow on. How could they see if fungi grow on left-out food? What other ideas do the children have? Why do they think these things? Devise an investigation.

Grow another fungus

Place an apple in a see-through container and cover with cling film. Watch what gradually happens. What do you notice? Usually the apple will shrivel. Before that it may go brown in parts, and then blue dots appear around the brown area. You have seen another fungus!

Hunt for algae

Look on the outside walls of buildings, on stone paths or wooden garden seats, particularly where it is damp. Can the children see any green patches? This is probably an algae. Look on tree trunks; often on one side, north facing, there are green patches on the bark.

Outcomes

After being involved in some of the activities about other living things children may have an appreciation of the many different forms of life. They should have grasped the concept that if an organism is not green in colour like plants, which make their food, and cannot move around to find food like animals do, it has to obtain its food in a ready made form by living on other living things that have food that the smaller organism can 'steal' and use. The children should be able to recognize fungi and be aware that some are poisonous to humans. They may now understand that 'germs' can be harmful to us and know simple precautions to take, such as hand washing. They may also realize that food needs protecting from being invaded by fungi and bacteria.

8 | Forces – pushes and pulls

Summary

Forces are pushes and pulls. We cannot see them but we can notice the effects of them. There are forces of friction, air resistance and gravity. Forces are balanced and unbalanced. When the pull and push are balanced there is no effect; whatever is experiencing the force does not move. When the forces are unbalanced there is movement. When something is not moving there are still forces acting upon the object. Forces make things speed up and slow down. In an object moving at constant speed, the forces are rebalanced. Many playground toys display forces in action, such as swings, slides and see saws. The wind is a force.

> ### Key words
>
> Force, push, pull, gravity, friction, balanced, twists, machines, slopes, ramps, screws, moving, constant speed, pulleys, work, wind, gravitational pull, Newtons, Newton metres, weight, mass, equal, opposite, space, floating, sinking, up thrust, torque, air pressure, planets, weightless, lever, pivot, fulcrum.

Big ideas

Measuring forces

Forces are measured in units called Newtons, named after Sir Isaac Newton (1642–1727). It was Newton who first described the force of gravity when (according to the story) he watched an apple fall to the ground from the tree under which he was sitting. In fact one Newton is about at the weight of one apple

What forces do

Forces change things; the speed of an object, the direction in which that object is moving and the shape of the object. Forces move in straight lines, and the direction in which a force moves is important. If, for example, a moving toy car hits something (that is a push force back at the car from what it hit) the direction in which the car was moving may then change as it 'bounces' off the object in a straight line, or stops. In the same way hitting a ball running across the floor changes the direction of movement of that ball. If a force is being transmitted through something like a rope or piece of string, the string has to be tight, in tension, or the force will not be transmitted.

Gravity

The force that Newton observed when the apple fell to the ground is the force of gravity, which acts towards the centre of the earth; always downwards. In fact it is this gravitational pull that gives objects weight; weight is how hard the earth is pulling that object. Earth's gravitational pull at ground level is about 10 Newtons (N) per kilogram (kg), so something with a mass of 1 kg weighs 10 N. Our mass does not change but our weight depends on the gravitational pull being experienced. If you were to weigh yourself on a weighing machine that simulates the gravity on other planets, such as Mars, you would have a different weight because each planet has its own specific gravitational pull. In space there is no gravity, which is why space men appear weightless in outer space and when an astronaut on the moon dropped a hammer and a feather from the same height they fell to the surface at the same time.

Gravity effects everything, but some objects have a stronger upthrust in the opposite direction; that is why a boat may float on water but may sink when a heavy load is added. Likewise, the upward thrust provided by the engines in an aeroplane overcomes the force of gravity and balloons float when the upthrust from the air is greater than the downwards pull of gravity. When a sheet of paper or piece of cardboard floats above the ground the up thrust of the air slows the downward fall. This can be compared with an object that experiences little air resistance such as a pencil, which will fall more quickly.

Balancing forces

If the forces acting on an object are equal/balanced, the object stays still, but if a larger push or pull force is applied, the object moves. If there is also a push and a pull in the same direction this is called a resultant force and the object moves in that direction with a total force value of the two forces added together. The object keeps moving and, if no other forces are applied to it, keeps moving at the same speed and in the same direction until the energy it has appears to run out and it stops.

Friction

Every action has an equal and opposite reaction: this is called Newton's third law. This means that when a child tries to push a toy car over a rough surface and the car does not move, the surface is providing the push-back force called friction. If the car is on a very smooth surface then there is hardly any push-back force, or friction, so very little force or push from the child is needed to make the car move.

Using forces everyday

A force has to be used to open things such as doors, drawers and cupboards. Some door handles have to be pushed down, a down force, while some have to be twisted in a similar way to lids of bottles and jars. This twisting action of a force is called a torque. Turning a door handle is applying torque, a twisting movement, and is how energy is transformed from one direction to another. Look at toys and see if there are any that have a twist and change the direction of the movement. The axle of a toy car shows this; the car is pushed forwards and the wheels go round but are attached to an axle, which also goes round and transmits the force to the other side of the toy vehicle.

Changing forces – simple machines

Forces can be transformed. Pulleys and levers do this. The mover uses a lever to move something heavy with less effort. Prising the lid off a tin with a spoon handle, for example, is using a simple lever. A heavy load can be lifted by a lighter load by putting the heavy load nearer the pivot on which the lever is resting, like on a see saw when an adult sits near the mid point (pivot) and the child sits right at the end of the see saw (lever). Effectively the child is sitting on a longer lever than the adult. Long levers can move heavier loads; this is called a first order lever. Lifting a wheelbarrow up with things in it is easier to push then lifting the things straight up. This time the pivot or fulcrum is at the end of the machine, the load is next to it, and the effort, the pull up, is at the end. This is a more complex lever and called a second order lever.

Making work easier using forces

Pushing a laden trolley up a ramp either a straight one or a zig zag one rather than straight up a very steep slope means the load (e.g. shopping trolley or luggage trolley) is pushed a much further distance but with less effort on the part of the person pushing. A string put over a pole to pull up a load at the other end of the string is really a lever with bend. The lever is the minute straight bit across the top of the pole. Pulley systems are seen in cranes and on sailing ships. The number of strings in a pulley system, as long as they are in tension, makes the effort of lifting the load in question as many times easier

8.1 The ladder acts as a ramp, a simple machine, making a slope that is easier to climb up than a vertical upright side.

as there are strings. A ladder sloped against a structure is a ramp effectively, as in many climbing sets. A slide is a shiny ramp too!

Moon, sea and tides

Celestial bodies have their own gravitational pull and this can affect other bodies to which they go near. Our moon, with its own different gravitational force, exerts an effect on the earth, which is seen by the tides of seas at either hemisphere. When the moon is nearer the earth than at other times of the year, high tides occur, and when it is furthest away and the pull is least, very low tides occur. The effect near the equator is much less all year round. The wind is a force. Wind is discussed further in Chapter 11.

Water pressure

Everything on earth is affected by its gravitational pull; hence, waterfalls flow downwards. Water takes the shape of what it is in, but is still pushing. Air too exerts pressure; the deeper under a body of water one goes, the greater the pressure. Air presses down on water so the water actually presses in all directions when the water is in a container. If there is a hole in the container the water is pressed out by the air pressure and the gravitational pull of the earth. When a jet of water is squirted it does not continue in a straight line but gradually curves towards the earth, as does anything thrown such as a ball or a rocket. What goes up must come down, while it stays within the gravitational pull of the earth.

Talking and doing

The following activities provide young learners with first-hand, hands-on experiences of forces. They will already have used forces in their everyday lives without realizing that, for example, opening a door by pulling is using a force. Pushing down the door handle or twisting it are also examples of using forces. As you work, point out the everyday push and pull actions that you and the children make.

Talking forces

Collect photographs and drawings of everyday forces. Take photographs of items around where you are working with the children or simple toys to show simple machines, such as screws, ramps, pulleys and slides. Find the toys that show some of these machines in action and put them on a 'machines' table. Tell the children the names of the items and the kind of simple machine in the toy such as screw, ramp, slide or pulley. Have items such as a screw, toy garage with ramp, slide or drive up to garage floors. Tell the children the names.

What goes up and down? Everyday forces

What forces do the children use and see every day? Ask them what things they push and what they pull. Why do they have to push and pull things?

Clothes and forces

What force do they use when putting on their clothes and shoes and socks? Pull or push? Suggest the children pretend to be dressing. Ask the children to say when they are pulling clothes and when they are pushing.

Squash it!

What happens if they put their foot down on something like a small empty cardboard box? What do the children think will happen? Why do they think this? What words do the children use to describe this? Push down? Lift up?

Have a few old boxes, such as empty cereal or tissue boxes. Invite the children to exert a push force on the box. They are applying a force! Making foot prints in snow, sand, mud or with a wet foot on a dry surface or sand is the result of the force of their body on the surface.

Sucks and squeezes

Ask the children how they squeeze toothpaste or something else from a tube. How do they suck up drink from a glass or carton? What happens if they blow instead? How do they get something, e.g. cereal, out of the packet? Shaking and squeezing are all pulls or pushes.

Going up!

Balloons filled with air or anything thrown up by the child goes upwards. Such actions are working opposite the force of gravity but eventually gravity 'wins' and the items stay on the ground or whatever surface they land upon. What can the children say about when things are dropped? Do they notice a pattern? Does the same thing always drop when they let it go? This is gathering evidence and seeing a pattern emerge.

Dropping things

What everyday items fall to the floor if dropped? What happens if they accidentally drop something? Where does it go? Use the language of dropping, including catching, breaking, falling and bouncing in your dialogue with the youngest learners.

Down and up

What things go up again after they have gone down? Ask the children what they think.

Bouncy balls do because the property of the material from which they are made causes the ball to bounce back up.

Dropping things – air resistance

Is there a difference in how long an object takes to drop to the floor compared with another kind of object? Try dropping a feather and a pencil. The feather has air resistance so takes longer. Find pictures or a film clip of the astronaut on the moon, who dropped a feather and a hammer. Why did the objects land at the same time?

Drop and see

What happens every time something is dropped?

Invite the children to show you what 'drop' means using a crayon or other small unbreakable items. What action do they have to do for dropping something?

Collect a few items from the toy box and have the child stand on the carpet and drop the items one by one, such as a crayon, a soft brick, a piece of paper and a piece of fabric. What happens? Does the object go up or down? Say the word that is applicable to them. Give them something non-breakable and small, such as a plastic bottle and ask them what they think will happen if they drop it. Find other objects and repeat, with the children making their predictions.

Wind

Let them feel the wind; can they talk about it? What words do they use? Where have they felt the wind? What is the wind like outside today? Is it a strong or mild wind? How do they decide on the strength? Can the children make air move to cause a wind? How? If they flap a piece of card, which kind works best; firm or floppy? How can they judge which is the 'best' wind? What do they mean by 'best'?

Pushes and pulls and lifts

Children need practical experiences of what forces do and the machines that humans use to make work easier. Provide experiences for your children of pushing and pulling things, some with wheels and some without.

Start with challenging them to point out things from every day that they need to push or pull to make work, such as pushing a door closed, pulling up the lid of a storage box, pulling open a draw or pulling a book off bookshelf or even their coat off a coat peg. How many such push and pull things are there in everyday life?

Encourage them to group their toys into those they can push, those they can pull and those to which they can do both.

When they have explored pushes and pulls, ask them in which direction do they push them? Can they control the direction? How?

Floating

Throw some light things, such a sponge ball, up in the air. What happens? Blow up some balloons and attach a string to them. Then let a balloon full of air go, but hold on to the string. What happens?

Leave a balloon on the ceiling. What happens after a while?

What happens when an unfilled balloon is thrown up in the air? Do balloons with differing amounts of air in them all float up as high as each other?

Helium-filled balloons such as children may have at parties rise higher and need a stronger pull to bring them down. Say 'Up' and then 'Down' as the children do the action.

Floating and sinking

Ask children that kinds of things will float in water, what kinds will sink and why. Once they have answered, carry out this experiment using some of the objects they named. Try a pencil, a sponge ball, a metal and plastic spoon, a pebble and an eraser. What happens? What happens if you put a plastic bottle or milk container with its lid screwed on into water? What happens if the children take off the lid and repeat the action? What is the difference? Do the children notice the water gradually going in the bottle, and that at some point the bottle sinks?

Boats

Toy boats and other containers and objects float in water. What makes them float and what makes them sink? Try making shapes in foil and find out which float. Put some cargo, e.g. centicubes, pieces of Lego or same-size pieces of modeling clay, in the foil boats. What happens if you keep on putting in 'loads'?

Salty water and floating

What happens to the toy boats in very salty water? Show the children salt and then show them water using the names. Add the salt to water and see what happens.

Find pictures of people floating in the Dead Sea. Explain that this is a sea with much more salt in than others. Explain that sea water is salty. The water we use to drink and wash and water in rivers and lakes and other water bodies such as ponds and puddles are not salty.

Salt water is denser than fresh water so has more upthrust working against the pull of gravity.

 ## Friction

After introducing toys with wheels, such as a toy vacuum cleaner, car or truck, ask if the children discover that the harder they push or pull, the more easily and/or faster the object will move? When they are pushing over a rough surface, do they find they need much more effort to make the toy move as the surface is pushing back at them?

Changing direction

Ask if the children can change the direction in which the wheeled toy moves. Can they make it move more quickly or slowly? What happens if it is on a rough surface? Will it move as easily? Why not? What kinds of surfaces would help the toy move more easily? Can the child make the toy move backwards; what do they have to do? These actions are all about pushes and pulls. Keep saying 'Push' and 'Pull' where appropriate.

Smooth or rough

What is rough? What is smooth? Can the children tell you what surfaces are smooth and what are rough in the learning area? How do they know?

Do the children notice that they have to pull or push harder when the truck (for example) is on a rough surface? Do the children think that it is easier to make a wheeled toy move across the smooth, hard playground surface than the same action on grass? Why do they think this? Encourage them to try and see if what they thought is what happens.

They probably decide that the different surfaces for moving toys – shiny, rough and smooth – require more or less force from them to pull or push the toy.

Slippery shoes

Look at different types of shoes and their soles and see which give them the firmest grip on a shiny, slippery surface. Sort them into groups of gripping shoes and sliding shoes. Talk about where you would wear each kind of shoe and why. What words could you use in this investigation?

Making it easier

Using simple machines makes work easier. Walking up a slope is easier than walking up steps or trying to climb a wall to get to the same height above ground. Children love playing on slides, but they have to climb up an often vertical ladder to reach the top of the slide so that they can come down again. The slide is a shiny ramp and requires less effort to come down.

Tight string; floppy string

For this activity children need to know what string is like (i.e. floppy or can be pulled tight) because it can be changed by applying a force to it. What can be done with floppy string? Tie a piece of string to a small box or folded piece of card. Can this item be pulled with floppy string? What does the child have to do to pull it?

If the child is pulling along a truck loaded with big bricks, for example, will the truck move if the string is floppy? What does the string have to be like for the truck to move? Does the string have to be taut, in tension?

Slide or steps?

Ask the children which is easier to do: climbing up the steps or coming down the slope of the slide?

No hands

Ask the children if they can move something upwards without lifting it up with their hands. What ideas do they have? What does upwards mean?

Ramps

Suggest that the children push a car from the floor level to the top of a low box without lifting it.

They will probably think of getting a piece of card and making a ramp. They can see this in toy garages.

Lifting and making work easier

There are ways of lifting something to get it somewhere higher that take less energy or effort from the lifter.

Ask the children to show you how they could achieve this. Suggest lifting a book or heavy toy from the floor to the table.

Lifting heavy things

Give the children the task of pulling things up, like lifting a bucket of sand up from the sand tray or a container of water, with the lid on, from a bucket to a nearby stool. What do the children work out for themselves?

The lifting becomes easier if the rope is put over a frame, such as over the back of a chair, with one end tied to a container like a small bucket that the item to be moved is loaded into. The child pulls on the other end of the string so the bucket, with its load, is pulled up. This way is easier than a straight lift; the effect of the same strength of pull is twice as great, thus making the lifting less difficult. This machine has effectively two strings in tension, acting like levers, but it makes lifting the bucket easier. All the time the string must be taut.

Ramps and screws

Another way of getting the object between levels is by using a ramp. Effectively you are making the distance up which the object moves further but less steep, so less hard work.

Children may have seen such ramps at supermarket exits or airports where they are provided to wheel luggage where there are steps.

Ramp and screw search

Look round the Foundation wing or nursery and see with the children whether there are any ramps or screws in the room or outside. Look at toys and doors. There may be a screw toy in the play area in the water tray, which when turned moves the water from one level to another.

A toy that may have ramps wrapped around it is a lighthouse. This is like a screw; the path around the lighthouse winds round and round the upright building. The path is a ramp wrapped round a central axis. It is a simple machine.

Some early learning toys for very young children are screws with nuts to screw onto them. Encourage children to play with such toys; for example, the toy garages with ramps. Ask them how a slide that you can make a marble run down could be made into a helter-skelter (you have to nick a piece of card to get it to turn). Look at pictures of helter-skelters in fairs. If you have large plastic screws show them how long the surface of the screw is by wrapping a piece of string around it and then laying it out.

Forces walk

Take the children on a forces walk round the area. Point to something and ask if this shows a force. Label the items with the words for older children and helpers in the room and outside. Have a picture of the force being used, such as a hand pulling down the door handle.

Photo journal of everyday forces

Ask children to identify when they are using a force, say to pull open the door or their tray. Make a collection of photographs of the children using forces and of the forces in your room. Make a 'big book' that you can use with a small group to talk about 'our forces and machines'.

Outcomes

Through being involved in some of the activities suggested and having everyday forces in action pointed out to them and talked about, children will appreciate the nature of forces and their importance in their lives. They do not need to know the physics theory at this age, but should have real hands-on experience of using forces in their everyday life and realize that they are doing so.

9 | Structures

Summary

All things have a shape, sometimes as a result of the material from which they are made. Shapes are everywhere: the bricks or other materials that construct buildings, shapes of the structures in bridges, packing materials, furniture, transport. Some shapes such as triangles and circular items are much stronger than other shapes. Children can investigate shapes with everyday items and materials, constructing new shapes and using already made ones. They can use different materials; some materials can change shape and some have different strengths when arranged in different ways, for example a tube made out of a piece of flat paper. Early years children need first-hand experience of playing at science and engineering using a variety of shapes constructed from a range of materials.

> ### Key words
>
> Shape, structure, materials, load, dimensional, stable, base, force, pliant, triangles, squares, circles, spheres, ellipses, hexagons, rectangles, polygons, pentagons, hollow, solid, three-dimensional, two-dimensional.

Big ideas

All things have shape. Some things have their own shape; others, like liquids, take the shape of the container in which they are constrained.

Shapes are everywhere

Shapes are everywhere; the bricks and other materials that construct buildings have a shape. There are shapes in the structures in bridges. Packing materials and furniture have a variety of shapes. Look for shapes in different forms of transport, such as the shape of lorries, trains and aeroplanes. What shapes are their doors, windows and wheels? What shapes are plates and mugs? There are shapes everywhere, all used in our everyday lives. Some shapes, such as triangles and circular items, are much stronger than other shapes.

Building with shapes

Shapes can be built on top of each other. The wider the base area of the construction the more stable it is, provided the weight (mass) of the materials is over the centre of gravity of the structure. Hollow shapes (squares, rectangles) tend to give way if weight is put on them but triangular hollow shapes and tubes are much stronger.

Grouping shapes

Grouping different shapes with different properties, such as two-dimensional and three-dimensional or different colours is the basis of categorization; giving the reasons why a shape has been allocated to a particular category is the foundation for argumentation skills, an essential part of learning science (see Chapter 1).

Some materials can change shape; applying a force can make the same amount of clay into a different shape. By modelling pliant materials they can be designed to do different jobs. A ball of clay is arranged in a different way to a slab of clay.

Different shapes made from the same material have different strengths when used to build or support things. Tubes are strong, as are triangles. Squares made as a hollow shape like a brick to hold something up are not by themselves very strong, but inserting a piece of folded card inside makes them stronger. You can make other 3D shapes and put 'triangles' inside, then test their strength by putting on a load – use masses, e.g. 10 g, the same each time on the different shapes.

Talking and doing

Exploring structures is an essential hands-on/minds-on activity. It requires everyday materials such as newspaper, card and cardboard boxes of various sizes as well as modelling clay and everyday utensils. Children may need to be encouraged to build structures with the materials. You may like to challenge them to build the highest tower or make a bridge across a gap to support a favourite item if they do not start investigating spontaneously. Working with these activities, observing and talking and asking questions, children should begin to appreciate various structures and that some shapes are more useful as strong supports than others.

Shapes

Making shapes

In their earliest years, a learner needs to play with clay and see that a force from them can change the shape of the lump of clay. Roll out clay with a rolling pin or similar or just by patting the clay with a hand. Try cutting out shapes with biscuit cutters, then roll the shape up into a ball by hand and apply a force and flatten the shape. Cut another shape.

What shapes are there?

Find and discuss basic shapes such as triangles, squares, circles, spheres, ellipses, hexagons and rectangles from early years toys.

Polygons – hexagons, pentagons

Cut out the outlines of these shapes in different sizes from card, thus producing a set of different-sized two-dimensional shapes that the children can sort in a variety of ways – e.g. all same shape but different sizes, all same size in one set.

More ways to sort shapes

Use different-coloured card for some of the shapes so colour as well as size and shape is an attribute that can be used in sorting. Use different thicknesses of card to add yet another feature with regards to which the shapes can be grouped. Ask children what their reasons were for sorting the shapes as they have done. Is there another way in which they could do this?

Naming shapes

Say the names as you show the shape. Can the children repeat the names?
    Can they pick out the correct shape from a collection when you say its name?
    What shapes are there in the play kitchen?

My best shape

Can they say which shape they like best and why?

Shape of things – look, name and match

Find some objects in the room such as a small box, a crayon and a book. Hold each one up in turn in front of a cut-out shape made of card or a plastic shape from a set of shapes to see if the object that is held up matches.

2D or 3D?

Use the three-dimensional shapes of early years' items. Mix three-dimensional shapes with the flat two-dimensional ones; this is yet another attribute in which shapes can be sorted.

Shapes all around – shape hunt in class

What different shapes can you find around? What are the shapes used for? What are they doing?

Shape walk inside and out

Take the children on a shape walk, starting with walking around the room; what shapes can be seen? Walk round the building inside, and then outside. Identify the shapes they find – stick a label on them with a picture of the shape drawn on.

Colour code shapes

Which colours would the children like to use to code the shapes? They may suggest, for example, red for circles, green for squares or yellow for triangles. Make a simple 'bird's eye' map of the room and draw the items of furniture. Have sticky coloured dots and then as they walk around the children could stick the coloured dot on the correct place on the map.

Shapes in plants

Take a nature walk; what shapes are the plants you see? Can you recognize any shapes? Are there any oval leaves? Any round leaves? Any round stems? Round fruits? Flowers whose outline is round? Any square stems?

Food container shapes

Find the shapes of different containers, such as cereal boxes, kitchen paper rolls, tins of food and packets of food. Which of these shapes are also in the children's learning area?

Food shapes

What different shapes are there in foods? What shape is a piece of sliced bread, different biscuits and vegetables? What shape are eggs in their shell and what are they like in shape when out of their shell?

Cutlery and crockery shapes

What shapes are knives and forks? What shapes make them up? What shapes are there in plates, cups and mugs and dishes? What other shapes are associated with eating?

Shapes in toys

What shapes are there in other toys? Can any children find circles? Can the children find squares and rectangles? How do they know that the shape is what they call it? What features does the item have that are shared with that shape?

Outside play shapes

What shapes are there in climbing frames?

Money shapes

What shapes are in play money? Say the names of the shapes.

9.1 Shapes are all round especially in buildings and play furniture. How many shapes can be found in the picture?

Other shapes everyday

Make a chart of shapes and put the relevant objects next to them.

Shapes and structure chart:

Shape	Items that shape in room	Items that shape inside	Items that shape outside
Square	Box mat	Tiles on floor	Window frames
Rectangle	Tissue box	Door frame	Letter box in door
Circle	Card tube	Punched hole in paper	Port hole window, end view of pipes
Triangle	Certain chocolate box	On toy crane arm	End of pitched roof
Ellipse (oval)	Toy egg	Mat	Window frame shape
Sphere	Ball	Door knob	Belisha beacon globe
Polygons e.g. hexagons	Toy 20p coin (7 sides)	Children's tables (hexagons)	Some small paving stones

Consider circular items such as bottles and containers for example. What is half a circle like? Look at spoons; they are rather like a circle.

Scales – rulers and measures

Produce a ruler or a tape measure and show them the scale. Talk about how using the same standard measure is very useful.

Hand measures

Ask the children to try using their hands as measures. Ask an adult to use their hand too. What did the children notice?

Box measure

Use a box as a measuring device; challenge the children to use their box to measure the length of a table with a straight edge, for example, or one side of a hexagonal table.

Box measures chart:

Name of measurer	Kind of box	How many box lengths in the table length?	How many hand widths?

Talk about it. Whose box was used the most times in the same length? Whose box had the smallest number of measures?

What other things could be used as measures? Children love using bottoms to measure length of benches!

Box and hands

Collect different sized and shaped boxes, such as cereal boxes, tissue boxes, cardboard boxes and other food boxes. Try measuring other things in the room with the boxes (measure everything with one size of box at a time) and then hands.

Box activities

Can the children fit boxes inside each other? Which are the smallest and largest? Which boxes stack best? Can the children build bridges of different materials and shapes?

Building piles of boxes

What is needed to build piles of boxes? Do the children work out that they need a wide base and make the pile narrower at top? These are centre of gravity issues.

All fall down!

Have some toy animals on a stout piece of card. Do they stand up? What happens if you shuffle the card? If you tilt the board to make a slope, what happens? When do the things fall over? Do they all fall at the same time?

Using shapes to build

Give each child five pieces of paper that are all the same size, e.g. 20 cm square pieces or playing-card size. What structures can they build by themselves? What structure can they build as a team of two, then of three, using their pooled cards?

How high can the structure get?

How can you measure the height of structures? Ask the children for ideas. Using centicubes is a very effective way or use the tens rods of Dienes apparatus to introduce standard measures.

Box towers

Let children select five boxes each and challenge them to build a tower that stays up.

Which boxes are best for building? What happens if the tower is started off using a small box at the base and larger, wider boxes are added to it? What happens if the largest box is used as the bottom of the tower? What sequence of boxes produces the a) tallest tower and b) the most stable?

How high is the tower? How wide at the base is each tower? Does the highest tower have the widest base?

Try tower building with large play blocks. What happens? How tall was the tower before it fell over?

Children with greater dexterity can use same-sized pieces of thin card to build. Encourage them to bend, roll or fold card. If they roll card to make a tube, you need a means of fastening the ends; pieces of sellotape work well. See if this applies if they fold it into a triangular shape, although some children just bend card to make a triangle using what it stands on as the base.

Tube towers

Try building a construction with tubes and flat pieces of card – cut card to different sizes and have tubes of different heights, e.g. kitchen towel tubes and toilet tissue tubes.

Shape towers

Encourage the tower builders to find other shapes and see what happens if they use them in their towers. What shapes and materials are in the largest, tallest tower?

Shapes of things

Why do different objects have different shapes?

Consider toy cars and lorries. Look at model aeroplanes. What features do these models of transport vehicles share? What is different, and why?

Do objects used for the same purposes always share the same features? Look at things that you can sit on. How many different things are there that can do the same kind of job? How are they the same? How are they different?

Eating utensils

Look at utensils that we use to eat with; knives, forks and spoons. What are they used for? How is each different from the rest? How are they the same? Compare plastic utensils with card ones, metal ones and with using hands.

Different footwear shapes

Have a collection of different kinds of footwear: trainers, wellingtons, sandals, flip flops and shoes. What features are the same? What are different?

Other shaped things

Look for items used to drink from and see what features are the same for each. What are different?

What other things perform the same function but are different in shape?

Bridges

Challenge children to use one sheet of plain paper or a page of newspaper to make a bridge across a small gap between two tables. The bridge needs to support a toy car, animal or plastic cup with a 5 gram mass. How can they make the paper stronger than just using it as a flat sheet?

Liquid

Have the same amount of water in various different-shaped containers, such as a shallow dish, a tall thin bottle, a mug and a plastic tube. Show the children how much water you put in. Provide them with the same amount of water and invite them to pour the water into the various containers. Does the water look like the same amount in each? What shape has the water taken?

Outcomes

After completing the activities the children should have experienced a variety of shapes and materials. They should have a fundamental understanding of the basic rules about shapes in terms of using them as bridges and supports and how they can be changed, depending on the material from which they are made.

---

10 | Changes

Summary

Things change: the weather, plants and animals. Living things change as they develop. For example, a seed grows into a plant, a baby human grows into an adult, and a caterpillar turns into a very different form as an adult butterfly or moth. Non-living things change too. For instance, in certain circumstances, water can change to a solid, ice, or a gas. Items can also join together to change into a new substance. If different substances are mixed together, such as sand and water, they can be separated by various methods such as filtering. Some things change when something happens to them and cannot be changed back. A cooked egg for instance is white round the yolk, compared to its yellowish see-through colour uncooked. However, some materials can change back into the substance they were before. For example, ice can change back into water when heated. Sounds change as does the light around us.

> ### Key words
>
> Solid, liquid, gas, change of state, mixers, separating, filtering, vapour, sound, light, electricity, metamorphosis, larva, imago, hibernate, dormant.

 ## Big ideas

Changes in everyday

Things in our world change. The amount of light we have changes, from a lot during the day when the sun shines, to there being hardly any at night, when the only light comes from the moon because our part of the earth has turned away from the sun. The weather changes; it may rain or be fine, be calm or windy, hot or cool, humid or dry.

Seasons

In the temperate parts of the world there are seasons, where the weather and the vegetation changes. In temperate climates like northern Europe or the northern hemisphere winters are cold and often snowy, whereas the summers are hot and frequently dry. Other parts of the world have seasons of very heavy rain called monsoons at certain times of the year after the weather has become very hot and humid.

Living things and change

Plants change according to seasons in temperate climes. Deciduous trees lose their leaves in the autumn after they have flowered and produced their fruit and when the weather is cooling. They are leafless in winter. New leaves appear first of all as buds in the spring.

Some animals hibernate during cold winters. Many mammals, animals with hair as fur, change the nature of their fur, it being thicker in winter. Some animals even change the colour of their fur according to the season; stoats for example have a white coat in winter with a black tip to the tail. In this form the animal is called ermine. In the summer their body covering is brown fur.

Animals tend to have their young in the spring. Before babies are born many animals change their behaviour and enter into courtship activities to attract a mate.

Changes as plants and animals grow up

Flowering plants change as they grow from a seed to a plant to an adult plant with leaves and buds that become flowers. The flower then withers, leaving a fruit full of seeds that may grow into a new plant, and the predictable cycle of change begins again. Seeds dry out over winter and in order to grow they need to absorb water. Dry seeds kept dry will not sprout.

Animals change too, from what they look like when they are born, to a young stage, then to a change stage and finally to the adult form. Some animals go through a complete change stage called complete metamorphosis before they become a very different-looking adult. A caterpillar changes into a chrysalis, which develops into the adult butterfly or moth. A beetle larva, which looks rather like a caterpillar, changes into pupa from which the animal emerges as a beetle.

Humans change too, from being a baby, through the young or child form, through adolescence or change stage, to the adult form. They show, like many other familiar animals such as cats, dogs, horses and sheep, incomplete metamorphosis. In incomplete metamorphosis the young resemble the adults in basic body form but not in proportions of the body; nor do they have the secondary sexual characteristics, such as body hair or breasts for female humans.

Change of state

Water changes state and can alter its form – from solid (ice), to liquid, to gas (steam). Steam can be seen rising from the spout of a boiling kettle, and is the process of heated, gaseous water reforming as a liquid. Some changes are reversible, for example chocolate melting, water vapour condensing on a cold surface and puddles evaporating into the air. Heating materials can bring about physical changes; the things melt and change what they look like. When candle wax gets hot when the candle is lit, it melts to form molten wax. Ice cream when heated becomes runny as the ice in it melts and changes to water.

Likewise, cooling materials down can also cause physical changes; cooling a liquid can turn it into a solid. This is seen when making ice cubes or ice-lollies in a freezer, for example, or when molten candle wax or runny chocolate cool and solidify. When some foods are cooled they become hard, like food taken directly from the freezer. Frozen food has to thaw out and the water in it become liquid again before we can eat it.

Mixtures

Sometimes different kinds of solids are found together in mixtures and need to be separated. This can be done by sieving; alternatively, if the solids are in a liquid, often the solid will sink to the bottom of the container (gravity working!) and the liquid can be poured off. This is decanting. Solids can be separated from liquids by a sieving process where the solution is poured through a material with holes in, such as a colander, to drain the water off. Examples of this sieving are straining peas with a sieve or colander from the water in the saucepan in which they have been cooked or tea strainers catching loose-leaf tea when the tea is poured out from a teapot. Filter paper can be used to filter liquid away from the solids, which stay on the paper, like coffee filters. Kitchen towel pieces can be used as a filter when put inside the inverted cut-down top of a soda bottle. If, however, the solid has dissolved in the liquid, like sugar put into hot water, filtering does not work. Then other methods have to be used. One way to take the liquid away from sugar dissolved in hot water is by heating it, causing the water to evaporate. This change is reversible; if changes are chemical, for example adding acid (vinegar) to sodium bicarbonate (baking soda), which makes bubbles of gas (carbon dioxide), they cannot be reversed. The gas cannot be put back into the bicarbonate powder.

Changing things permanently

Chemical change is when materials used break down and are permanently changed into something else. Food items are cooked and in this way we change our food, e.g. potatoes change from hard to soft pieces. Some foods change colour when they are cooked: fried meat becomes darker and white rice, which is hard before it is cooked, becomes soft and white. Wood and paper burn to ash, and burnt bread becomes burnt toast with black carbon. Cooking is all about heating cold substances, which then change, as in mixing flour, milk and eggs and making a new substance from the constituents such as a cake. When eggs are cooked they change and cannot be changed back to the raw egg state. Oxygen reacts with some other chemicals in cut surfaces of apples and potatoes and turns the whitish surface brown.

Sound

Sounds are part of our lives. Our world is noisy, but the noises change. Sound happens when something vibrates, for example a man using a pneumatic drill on a hard substance. Sounds move through the air or other materials and make the air vibrate. In outer space, where there is no air, there is no sound because there is nothing to vibrate. The vibrating air reaches our eardrums (and the sense receptor of other animals) and causes them to vibrate; this movement sends nerve signals to the brain, which interprets the noise. Grasshoppers have little spines on their largest hind legs that they rub together to make a noise. The more energy in the sound vibrations, the louder that noise is, for example hitting a drum gently to make a quiet sound or forcefully for a louder noise.

Light

Our daily world is light but night is dark. Shutting out the light makes it dark. Blocking the light source can create a shadow, as the light cannot pass through an object in front of the light source. When this happens the shadow is formed in front of the object, on the side away from the light source. One of the easiest changes to observe is the action of a switch. Most switches, other than dimmer switches, are either on or off. Whatever the switch controls does not operate when the switch is off, rather like a door that is either shut or open. Electricity and the switches on wall sockets or larger equipment seem to have a tremendous attraction for young children, who will happily sit by a socket switch pushing it up and down, on and off. Pushing a switch to 'on' connects the electric circuit so electricity flows. When the circuit is complete, the light goes on. When the circuit is broken, when the switch is put in the 'off' position, the light goes out. Electricity is stored in batteries, which are used as energy sources for many toys and household things including torches, clocks and remote controls for gadgets such as televisions.

Talking and doing

Change is part of everyday life, so much so that we take it for granted and often do not notice it. The activities in this chapter seek to help children recognize everyday changes and some yearly ones. Children can, for example, watch changes in weather, or how plants change with time and certain conditions, such as lack of water or low temperatures. They can explore the different sounds that they hear everyday and the ways in which sounds vary. Sounds can be made and children can explore ways in which they can make them too.

On and off

Find items that have switches that the children can just switch on and off. Plug socket covers that they can hold in their hand can be used and some toys have a switch built into them. On and off is similar to up and down (forces), which can be shown with straight door handles. Torches give satisfactory 'ons' and 'offs' because there is a response to the switching. Using the remote controls of the actual switch for various gadgets pleases children. Say 'on' and 'off' to them at the appropriate times.

Night and day changes in the light

Ask if there is light all day and night. What makes night? Point out that there is light in the daytime but very little at night. The sun does not go on and off like a light. The earth moves round on itself so that at night when we are facing away from the sun the light does not reach us.

Shadows

What happens when the child stands on a pavement, drive or playground when the sun is shining at them? They block the light from reaching the surface behind them and a shadow is formed. What colour is it? Why? What space is it? Does it stay still when the child moves?

Shadow stick

Put a stick in the ground and mark with chalk, a piece of tape, string or several little stones where the line of the stick's shadow is. Go back later and see if the shadow has stayed in the same place or not. Take photographs of the sundial and its shadow at different times of the day.

Making light

Find a light source, such as a torch, and shine the beam of light (usually after the children have played with on and off and seen the results of both actions) at a blank wall. Ask the children what would happen if they place their hand in the way of the light; would a shadow be formed? Young children seem to enjoy blocking the light as much as they enjoy switching the light source on and off!

Seasons

Mention what the weather is and then say which season it currently is. For example, in summer you could say the days are longer, and when the days later become shorter proportionally the nights become longer.

Day length

Talk about day length and hours of the day with the children. In winter do they get up and go to bed in the dark? What happens in summer? Short day length in temperate climates is associated with winter when deciduous plants lose their leaves, which return in the spring.

Signs of spring

In spring as days get warmer and longer you can see the green tips of the leaves of bulbs peeping through the soil where before there was no plant showing. Later, the plants produce flowers (such as the catkins of hazel and willow trees) followed by leaves. Plant bulbs in the autumn in a bowl and watch what happens to the surface of the bowl in spring when you bring the bowl from a dark cupboard.

What animals and plants can be seen today? Make a photo diary

Make a point of talking about the everyday plants and animals that are around where you are. Notice at intervals whether these things change. Ask the children and provide them with the vocabulary to describe what they see and what has changed.

Recording change

Taking photographs with the children of something that changes, like an apple tree, and making a photo journal is a useful activity. Young children have to learn about the seasons. The apples on the apple tree fascinated my eldest grandson when he was four one summer. When he came at New Year he asked to go outside and rushed off to the apple tree to see the apples. He was astounded that there were no apples there, and what was more, no leaves either! He was learning through observations that the tree changed. Next spring we showed him the flowers and where the apple formed as the fruit behind the petals.

Photo journals

You could, with the children, make individual, group or class photo journals of the garden in general or particular plants they like for the year. New children can refer to previous journals to notice what has changed and whether they see what other children saw before them.

Weather

Weather charts

Talk about the weather each day, describing the conditions using weather words such as rain, fine, sun, cloudy, hot, cold, storms, wind, thunder and lightning.

Weather symbols

Make a chart with symbols attached to magnets (adapt fridge magnets) and have the children decide which symbol best fits the weather on that day.

Clothes for weather

What clothes would be sensible to wear according to the weather today? Why? What clothes are best for when it is hot, cold, rainy or windy? Why?

Effect of weather

What effects do the different kinds of weather have on people? On the ground? On animals and plants? Talk about the activities one does each day and how they are affected by the weather.

Seeds and change

Look at some seeds out of a packet or those collected from plants in the summer and kept. Will they grow?

Leave them on a dish for a few days in the light. Leave a few similar seeds in a dish in the same position but with water. Ask the children what they think will happen. What does happen? Were the children correct in their predictions?

Change from seed to plant

Plant fast-growing seeds such as mung beans, which can be bought at the supermarket, or peas inside a see-through plastic beaker with a piece of kitchen towel rolled up inside lining the beaker, but with the seed between the wall and the towel. Pour a small amount of water in the bottom so that the paper soaks it up. The seeds must have been soaked first so they are no longer hard.

Taking up water by seeds

How much water is required to trigger the change from a dried seed to one ready to germinate?

Soak a few dried peas for 24 hours and then compare the soaked ones with the dried ones. What is different? What has changed? Unless a seed is soaked dry seeds will not grow. Try it!

Changing seed

Ask what the seed looks like and make a photo journal. Look each day and take photographs of the seed. What happens? Ask the children to say what is happening. What has changed? The plant is developing from the seed, what it looks like changes (see Figure 6.2).

Apples and potatoes change colour

Put a freshly-cut slice of apple or potato on a plate exposed to the open air. Ask the children to keep going to look at it and say what colour it is. Take photographs and keep them so you can compare the change in colour over time. The whitish surface gradually turns brown. This is a chemical reaction, like the yellowish runny part of a raw egg turning white and more solid when it is cooked.

Animals

Grown ups and babies

Talk about how animals change. How are the children different from you? Humans change from babies that cannot walk to adults that can and are much bigger.

All animals change. Caterpillars change into butterflies or moths and mealworm larvae change into beetles. Kittens and puppies grow into adult animals with a slightly different form. What do the children notice about the changes that the adult has undergone compared to the young form?

Lambs (young sheep) look somewhat different from adult sheep (ewes are what you will probably see, rams have horns). Ask children how the lambs are like their mothers and how they are different.

Chicks hatch from eggs and look very different from adult hens and cockerels. In the spring some farms and nature centres hatch chicks so children can see their young form and if they keep hens the adult form to which they will change.

Sounds

What sounds can be made that can be heard well or hardly at all? Ask the children to turn round so they cannot see you. Make a soft sound, such as blowing a piece of paper, and ask whether it is loud or quiet. Make a loud sound, such as clapping your hands or banging a lid with a large wooden spoon, then repeat the action with a metal spoon or knock two sticks together.

My sounds

Ask what sounds they remember hearing during the day or night and talk about them. You could make a rap.

Liked sounds

Do children have special sounds that they like? What are they, and why do the children like them? Are they the same sounds for different children?

Disliked sounds

What sounds do the children dislike? Why? Where do they hear them?

Making sounds

What ways can the children think of to make sounds? For example, they could hold a piece of computer paper in front of their mouth and hum into it.

Comb and paper instrument

Make a comb and paper musical instrument by using small plastic combs covered with shiny paper, thin greaseproof paper or a piece of computer paper. Put the comb and paper between the lips and hum onto the paper. What happens? What does it feel like? The children have made vibrations.

Glass instrument

Try filling different-sized glass jars with the same level of water, or use the same-sized jars or bottle with different amounts of water in them. Tap the side of each glass or jar in turn with a spoon. What happens?

How are loud are sounds made from drums, tambourines, whistles, xylophones, reorders, guitars, maracas?

How could children design their own music instruments?

Make noises using their bodies

What noises can they make just using themselves? For example, clapping, singing, stamping or blowing.

Mixtures and solutions

Some substances dissolve in others, such as sugar in warm water. How can you get the sugar back from the water? Try putting a small amount of the sugar solution in a saucer or other shallow dish and place on a windowsill or a flat surface near a heat source. The water will evaporate leaving some sugar, or a white substance.

Separating solids from liquids

Sometimes, a solid gets into a liquid and someone wants to get it out again. How can this happen? Ask the children. Give them a bowl of water with some plastic cubes floating on the top and some pebbles at the bottom of the bowl. What are their ideas?

Some suggestions

Perhaps solids that float can be picked out with a little net or small sieve. The pebbles can be scooped up or picked out with long plastic forceps. The water could be drained off into another container. Are these solutions the children had? Let them try for themselves.

No fingers!

Try floating different-sized objects in a bowl of water and challenge the children to devise ways of getting these solids out of the water without directly using their fingers.

A problem

Oh dear! How can the children separate the sand from water into which it has mistakenly been poured?

Pose the question and ask them what can be done.

The most obvious method to us is to decant the liquid by just pouring it off. What ideas do the children have? Let them try them out and review them.

Spread it out

An alternative, which takes longer, would be to spread the sand and water out on a tray and leave in warm place until all the water has evaporated.

Filters

Yet another solution would be to make a filtering system with a filter paper inside the funnel (from a cut-down inverted top of a soda bottle) and pour the stirred-up mixture into the funnel. The sand should stay on the filter paper (or folded kitchen towel) and the water pass through into the receptacle below, the bottom of the bottle. This is filtering.

Water through sand

What happens if water is poured through a layer of sand? Spread some sand over the surface of a sieve and invite the children to find out what happens if they pour water onto it. What do they think will happen? The water should pass through the sieve to be collected in a container underneath. The sand stays on the sieve (make sure the holes of the sieve are not large enough for the sand to pass through too). You could investigate sieves with different sized holes/mesh for children to experience the effect of different sized holes on sieving/sorting.

Cleaning dirty water

You could ask children how they could clean dirty water. They could pass the water through sand; this principle is used in water treatment works. Put the sand inside a tube (a cut-down soda bottle), which is held over a container. Pour dirty water (stir in some soil, or coffee) in at the top of the column and watch the colour of the water when it has trickled through the sand.

Add different sized solids to a container to make a mixture of, for example, centi-cubes, card coins, dried peas or beads. How can they be sorted back into groups? What do the children suggest?

Sorting coins

Using just the card money can present an interesting challenge. How can the different denominations of coin be sorted? Children usually invent a series of sieves in response to this challenge, starting with larger holes and gradually getting smaller in diameter as the larger items are kept behind.

Outcomes

Changes are all around and it is important in a child's learning experiences that s/he appreciates that some things remain the same while others do not. Both plants and animals change, as does the weather and the clothes we wear. Through talking and doing the activities suggested here, and more that you and the children think up, they will gain experience of the changes that happen. One of the important things for them to realize is that they too change, in how they feel, act and their appearance over time. Such talk also leads into personal and social education.

11 | Materials

Summary

Materials are all around. Some are made from naturally occurring substances from living organisms such as silk from silk worms, wool from sheep and other animals, cotton from the cotton plant and ropes from jute. Many everyday items are made from wood or stone, metals and non-metals. However, all things are made up of very small particles that join together, called molecules, and can be classified as solid, liquid or gas. Materials have differing properties depending on the small particles from which they are made. Some materials thrown away as rubbish are biodegradable and some are not biodegradable.

> ### Key words
>
> Solid, liquid, gas, change, absorb, glass, synthetics, polymers, plastics, magnets, attract, repel, surface tension, floating, sinking, density, insulators, mirrors, light, compounds, evaporating, soak, waterproof, molecules, transparent, reflect, metals, acids, react, solutions, change of state, carbohydrate, sugar, sucrose.

Big ideas

Different states

Substances may be solid, liquid or gas, different forms of the same substance. These are called the states of matter. Take the states of water, for example; the solid form, ice, can change into liquid water when heated, and when heated further turns into a gas, which for water is water vapour. This gas condenses and changes back to liquid water on contact with cooler air. If frozen, the liquid water changes back to the solid form, ice.

Most of what we see are solids. All materials are made of particles; the smallest particles are called elements, which are the substances on this earth that cannot be broken down any smaller. There are two sorts, known as metals and non-metals. Metals conduct electricity whereas non-metals do not very well. Most metals react with acids (vinegar is an acid, for example, used to make gases). This is chemistry and in chemical reactions elements react together to make substances called compounds, which also react together in certain combinations. They change into something else made from the elements.

Molecules make up everything

All living things are made of chemicals produced by chemical reactions; in a reaction nothing is destroyed, just rearranged. Molecules are held together by chemical bonds. When small molecules join together to make longer chains of molecules they are known as polymers, sometimes called plastics. They are an important material because they do not crumble, decay or rust. Some materials are very shiny and reflect light; some are smooth and some are rough; some materials are hard; others are soft and come in various colours. Other materials make a noise when knocked against something hard while others do not – it all depends on their properties. Some materials are good conductors of heat, such as metals, while others, such as wood, are not; a useful thing to know when cooking and wanting to stir the contents of a saucepan. A metal spoon conducts heat and the handle becomes very hot!

Using materials

We humans use substances called materials to make things in our world, for example wood, metals, polymers (compounds with many small repeating molecules) and glass. Some fabrics such as nylon and polyester are man-made and called synthetic. They are made from raw materials quite unlike the end product. Synthetic materials do not disappear as natural things do. The waste, thrown away by humans, can cause many problems as to how it should be disposed of. Other materials such as wool, linen, silk and leather are naturally occurring from plants and animals and through things humans do to them are turned into materials for use. Other organisms, such as birds that make nests using twigs and grass from plants, may also use materials in their lives.

Properties of materials

Different materials have different properties that dictate for what they are used. Steel, a metal, is strong so is best used to make things such as girders for buildings or car bodies. Glass is transparent so is useful for windows in buildings and so on so that people can see outside while protecting the inside from the elements. Wood can be used for construction as well as burnt for fuel.

Mirrors

Some materials are shiny and reflect light. Glass with silver paint behind it forms a mirror, as does the foil used in kitchens. Mirrors reflect light and light travels in straight lines. When an object is in the way of the beam of light a shadow is formed behind the object. Using mirrors to reflect light from one surface to another enables you to see around corners or over the heads of people, as in periscopes.

Insulation

Other materials are called insulators and keep heat or cold in; for example tea cosies or gloves keeping heat in or cool packs to keep frozen food cold. Other materials are waterproof or can be made so, as when a wax crayon is used to cover a piece of paper.

Liquids

Liquids flow. They are fluids but not all fluids are liquids. Liquids take the shape of the vessel in which they are contained. If they are not in the container they flow without a shape except that made by their surface tension. Liquids have surface tension and almost seem to have a skin, which lets some items, such as a needle, or some animals heavier than water to move across this surface. Surface tension is responsible for droplets of water when water runs on a waxy surface and causes raindrops. If oil and water are mixed and then separated out there is an interface between them caused by the different surface tensions. The spherical shape of a bubble is due to surface tension. Liquids, like gases, flow so these are both referred to as fluids. Things called surfactants reduce surface tensions and detergents act on these causing little fat globules to form. If oil, e.g. cooking oil, is mixed with water a suspension occurs, causing small globules of oil in the water.

Forming compounds

Compounds are made from two or more chemical elements that have come together. These elements can be separated again by chemical reactions, but not by physical methods such as filtering (unlike the parts that make up a mixture). Sea salt or cooking salt is made up of two elements: sodium and chloride. Sugar, which is a carbohydrate called sucrose, is made of two glucose molecules. Each of these molecules is made up of 6 carbon, 12 hydrogen and 6 oxygen atoms. Two molecules of glucose joined together form sucrose.

Sucrose dissolves in water. Cold water will not let as much sugar dissolve in it as will warm water. Stirring a solution increases the amount of substance that will dissolve. If hot solutions are cooled, some of the substance dissolved in the liquid, e.g. salt or sugar, reappears as it comes out of solution. If 10 ml of vinegar (an acid) is added to a teaspoonful of bicarbonate of soda in a beaker, bubbles are formed; this is carbon dioxide gas.

Evaporation

If a liquid mixture is heated, the liquid evaporates, leaving the salt in it as crystals. Water evaporates from its surface as can be seen when puddles in the playground dry out, leaving behind a mark of whatever was in the water. Boiling the whole body of liquid also causes evaporation, for example when a kettle boils dry.

Gases

Around our earth is a layer of gases called the atmosphere. Gases are made up of molecules but there are far fewer in gases than there are in liquids and fewer still than there are in solids. If heated, solids turn into gases and few can be smelt. Hydrogen sulphide gas is one that does have a smell. It is the smell of rotting eggs or stink bombs. Gases can rarely be seen unless they are coloured. When water is heated the gas is seen as the colourless gas just beyond the spout of the kettle; it is not the steam, which is water vapour as the gas is cooled and turns back to water.

Talking and doing

Many activities in this materials section are, in fact, about change.

The activities suggested introduce early learners to real experiences of different materials. Children need first-hand experiences and to understand the feel of appropriate materials such as cloth, paper, wood and plastic and the shapes of soft containers such as cloth bags, which can change according to the material put inside them. The material still feels soft but the item inside gives it a shape. Other containers made from hard materials cannot be changed easily. Some materials bend, some are rigid, some are soft and flexible while others are harder in nature. Children can experience the fact that they can change the shape of some materials such as clay and water through the shape of the container in which they are placed. Some materials are dull, yet others are shiny. Some materials are magnetic and attract certain materials. Sometimes magnets attract each other, yet at other times, if placed differently, push or repel the same magnet.

Liquids

Children need to have practice at feeling water and what it can do – splash, run and wet things. They need to be able to pour from one container to another including larger and smaller containers. Does the same amount of water in a large container fit into a smaller container? Provide different-sized containers and ask children what happens if they pour the water from a tall, thin container into a wide, flatter container. Provide containers of different diameters and depths. A wide dish for instance looks like it contains a larger amount of water because it covers a wider area, but the volume of water is in fact the same as it was in the first container from which it was poured.

Pouring

Children can try pouring different kinds of liquids, such as cooking oil and mayonnaise, to investigate viscosity. They can also try mixing liquids, say oil and water, and seeing what happens.

Solids

Children need to understand what a solid in everyday terms is like. What does it look like? What does it feel like? What is solid in your learning room? Take a 'solids walk'. Look, touch, feel and tap furniture and other things; sort them into solids and non-solids. Talk about them using the solid words.

Solid feel

The children really need to feel solids. What do they feel like? What can they do?

Have a collection of solids, e.g. sand, a pebble, a stone or brick, toy bricks (foam and plastic), a wooden spoon, a plastic box, a piece of paper, a piece of wool, string, a mirror (unbreakable), an earthenware cup, a plastic cup, a drinking glass, pieces of fabric and toy cars. Ask the children to sort them.

How do the children sort them? What are their reasons?

Do they sort according to properties, such as soft and hard, or according to colour, e.g. toy red brick and soft red brick, colour red brick and red fabric with objects that are not red in another set?

A runny solid

Sand is lots of little solid bits. What does it do? What does it feel like, look like, sound like in a plastic cup when shaken? Can you pour it? What happens if you put a small amount of water into a small amount of sand? Does it then still do all the things you have just done with the dry sand?

Noisy solids

Do solids make a noise? How can you get them to do so? What do the children think? Ask the children to try tapping them with their hand. What else do they suggest?

Does the noise vary depending on what solid they are tapping and with what sort of solid they are tapping it? Does a piece of fabric make a noise when tapped into a solid such as the table?

Materials for the job

Give children the name of the materials from which everyday things are made. Collect together items such as a plastic spoon, glass jar, plastic beaker, card beaker, plastic bottle, wooden spoon, wooden board, paper bag, book, fabrics, wool, linen, silk, fur (synthetic if you prefer), stone, brick, tile, mug, string, plastic and paper drinking straws, kitchen foil, kitchen towel, tissue, wellington boots, trainers, flip flops and some metal cutlery.

Using solids

Ask the children what each item is. What is each used for? Why, for example, is a mug not made of fabric or paper and the spoon not made of string?

Waterproof and water droplets

What is a droplet? Can you make droplets? Use pipettes, medicine droppers or medicine syringes (5 ml) to make drops. What happens if you squeeze a dropper with air in it? What happens if you do that when the end of the dropper is under water? What happens if you have water in the dropper and squeeze (aim at a dish)? If you squeeze the top hard what happens? What happens if the top is squeezed slowly? What happens to a drop when it lands on a saucer? A piece of kitchen towel? A piece of fabric, such as a tea towel? Can the children get a drop to run down a hard surface (e.g. the back of a plate)?

Drops on skin

What happens when a few drops of water go on our skin? Ask the children what they have noticed, then try out dripping a couple of drops.

Raindrops in a puddle

What happens when raindrops hit a puddle? Try simulating rain with a dropper of water onto a bowl of water.

Some drops don't mix

What happens if you drip a drop of vinegar into a saucer of cooking oil? Do they mix? What happens if you drop water into oil?

Paper and drops

What happens if you drop some water onto a piece of paper? What happens to the drop of water? What happens if you cover a patch of the paper with a wax crayon and then drop some water on (use a medicine syringe or a straw as a dropper if you do not have one)? Use a small watering can outside to pour some water on the outside surface of an open umbrella. What happens? What happens to a drop of water on a Wellington boot or rain hat? What happens if you put a drop of water on a piece of shiny fabric or on foil?

Inquiry drops

Have some waxed paper and foil. What happens if water drops onto these surfaces? Try it and see. Use a dropper or squashy bottle; you have to push (using a force to get the water out). It drops some water. Watch what happens to it. Drop water onto an open umbrella. What is the job of umbrellas? How do they do this? What happens to us when it rains and we wear our rain clothes? What happens to our clothes if they are waterproof? Try dropping water onto cloth and paper towels and see what happens. What is the difference?

Your special skin

What can the children deduce about their skin having investigated waterproof materials? Why is this a useful characteristic for us to have? Ask the children whether they stay the same size and shape when in water, or if they take in water through their skin and swell up?

What shape is water?

Look at water in a jug. What does it do? What is it like? What words can the children think of to describe the water's movement and shape? What does it feel like? Does it smell? What colour is it? What happens when you look through the sides of a clear container with water inside it? Can you see through it or not? Can you make a drop of water?

Is it the same volume? Visual puzzle

What happens to the shape if you empty the jug onto a large flat dish or tray (make sure you have a large enough tray)? Encourage the children to watch as you pour out the water; where does it go? It makes a puddle if the tray is much larger than the amount of water poured out. If the water is poured into a small square container, what does its shape it look like?

Hot and cold solid liquids

What happens after a while if you leave out an ice cube in a dish or some ice packs from the medical centre? Can you speed up the process? What would you have to do?

Slow down meltdown

How can you slow down the melting process by keeping the cold in and the heat out? What ideas do children have? Try them out.

Some materials stop most of the heat inside from passing through them. What if a beaker has contents that make it very cold to hold; what can you do so you can hold it? Try to collect some of the card or holders that coffee stalls put round hot card coffee cups.

Surface tension

Surface floating

Ask children what they think will happen if you sprinkle or drop things on the surface of a beaker of water. What should they sprinkle?

Try sugar granules, salt, ground pepper, a piece of cloth and a piece of string. What happens? Look through the side of the beaker too and watch what happens. Talk about it and work out why.

Pepper and cotton are every light and do not break through the skin or meniscus, so they float on top of the water.

Walking on water

If you have a pond to look at in summer you may see pond skaters looking as though they are doing just that, skating over the source of the water.

Moving fat

Put some oil (e.g. cooking oil) on a plate and add some water. What happens? Now add a squirt of washing up liquid (detergent). What happens? This phenomenon is all to do with surface tension. When do we use washing up liquid? What do we use it for?

Blowing bubbles

Use bubble mixture and the wire rings and blow bubbles. How do the children make bubbles? What do they do? What happens to the bubbles? What shape are they and what colour? Are they all the same size? Where do they go? How long do they stay as bubbles?

Where else do you see bubbles? Try making bubbles with different solutions and other things that children can think of. Bubbles have air trapped inside them.

Salt and sugar water

Why do people stir their tea or coffee if they have sugar in it? What happens if they don't stir it?

What happens when you add spoonfuls of salt to a see-through beaker or plastic glass of water? Look through the side of the beaker after each spoonful. Some salt dissolves in the water.

Stirring it up

If a heap of salt or sugar forms on the bottom of the beaker, have the children any ideas as how you could make it disappear?

If they don't, suggest that stirring the mixture with a spoon might help.

Warming the water gently by standing in a bowl of hot water or adding some hot water will also increase rate of dissolving. Try the activity again, this time with warm water and see if more salt or sugar dissolves first before stirring.

Magnets – finding out what is attracted and what is not

Collect some fridge magnets and give one to each child. Challenge them to find out what the magnet does. They intuitively go to stick it on things and usually find it will stay on metal things but not on non-metals such as wood, plastic, glass or fabrics.

Ask him or her to tell each together what they find out. What happens if the two fridge magnets are put together? Some toys have magnets, for example carriages of a train set whose couplings are magnets or wobbly men that dance on a turntable.

Glass – what is it like and how do we use it?

When can the children see out of the window? What happens if a small patch of the window glass is painted with black (washable) paint? Can the children see through a solid door made of wood or metal? What is special about the window glass? The word transparent is one they relish saying!

Mirrors and shiny things

Mirrors are glass with silver backing, Can the children see through a mirror? What do they see when they look into it?

Mirror touch

Can they touch their nose? Their left ear? Their right ear? What does the action look like in the mirror?

Mirror writing

What happens if you hold a piece of writing up to the mirror? What does it look like in the mirror? Write each child's name out on a piece of card; let the child look at their name without the mirror and then look at their name as it appears in the mirror.

Can they use a mirror to shine a light on something?

Can the children use mirrors in such a way so they can see above something (such as a book case) or round a corner? Let them play with several mirrors; standing them in pieces of modelling clay is useful so the mirrors are upright. If you have a toy periscope you can show them that inside there are two mirrors bouncing light off each other. If the children have a torch they can try using the mirror to shine the light onto other things, like the wall or a piece of paper held up as a screen.

Materials and temperature

Some materials keep heat in and some keep cold in.

Try asking the children what happens if they leave an ice cube in a dish. What do they think? How can they find out if their predictions happen? Try, watch and see.

Insulation

Ask the children how they could stop the cube from melting, other than putting it back in the freezer (if someone suggests this). How can you keep the cold in or the heat from getting at the ice cube? Suggest, if they don't think of it, wrapping it up in different materials – newspaper, cotton, wool, plastics or cool bag.

How can you make the ice cube change into water quickly?

Cooking pots

What is best to use when cooking vegetables? Is a paper container any good? What about wood? What about plastic? What about metal? What containers do they see being used? Saucepans, dishes?

Stirring the cooking

Put a metal spoon into a container of warm water (not boiling!) alongside wooden spoons. Touch the tops of the handles every so often; what happens? You can put a lump of sandwich spread on the end of each handle and watch what happens.

Clothes and weather

What kinds of clothes do people in different countries wear? What would the children say they would wear in a hot desert or sandy place with sand blowing about?

What would they want to wear in a very cold and snowy place where they had to walk on snow?

Walking on snow and sand

What happens if you walk on snow in ordinary shoes? How could you stop sinking in?

Sand walk

Ask the children happens when people walk on sand. How can you change what happens? Find out why camels don't sink into the sand when they walk.

Keeping warm

How do the children keep warm?

What clothes do the children use to keep heat in? What part of them becomes cold most easily? What clothes can they wear on their heads, their nose, their ears, their hands and their bodies to keep warm?

Keeping cool – fans and shades

What do the children do to keep cool when it is hot?

How else can the children cool down? Make some fans and see what effect that has.

Design and make a parasol or sunshade, or a sun hat.

Clothes for hot weather

What do the children think they would wear if it is hot and they wanted to let heat out?

Collage of clothes

Obtain magazines and catalogues with clothes. Help children choose clothes for hot, cold and wet weather. Cut out pictures and ask them to select hot weather clothes, cold weather clothes and wet weather clothes. Make a mobile of weather clothes by tying the pictures to a wire coat hanger and hanging up the mobile.

Outcomes

Materials is a vast subject, ranging from fabrics made from chemicals such as nylon and polyester to naturally-occurring items such as silk, wool, wood and stone to liquids, gases, mirrors and magnets. Through working with some of the activities suggested in this chapter, young children will have real experiences of the variety of materials in their everyday world, which will lay a firm basis for future science learning.

12

The built environment

Summary

Buildings have a number of roles and are constructed from a variety of materials, often depending on where they are built and for what purpose. Humans have altered the landscape by cutting down trees and ploughing the land as well as constructing dwellings. The pathways that people built have become paved roads constructed from hard materials rather than mud, often in towns with sidewalks or pavements and with bridges for people to cross away from traffic. People paint signs on the road and put items on them such as traffic lights, and things on the pavements such as seats and postboxes. Buildings have particular functions such as shops for various produce, homes, hospitals, service stations and leisure centres. The insides of buildings are also the built environment.

> ### Key words
>
> Environment, buildings, vehicles, cars, bicycles, lorries, buses, vans, trains, aeroplanes, prams, scooters, transport, bricks, stones, cement, boats, ships, fields, hedges, wood, paint, furniture, seats, lampposts, bins, walls, plant pots, roads, pavements, gardens, fences, signs, postboxes, gates, railings, shelter, traffic lights, trees, plants, rivers, canals, maps, rooms.

Big ideas

Humans have changed the world

We humans live in a world that has been greatly altered from the natural state. Through various activities we have changed the way much of it looks. In the developed world this is particularly pronounced, as roads cover the earth as well as pavements and buildings constructed from wood and stone or human-made materials such as cement and steel. Cement is made from limestone, calcium, silicon, iron and aluminium, plus lesser amounts of other ingredients. Concrete contains cement plus sand and gravel. Cement binds the sand and gravel or crushed rock together to form concrete.

Nowadays, particularly in towns, people who had front gardens with lawns and flowerbeds are covering them over to provide hard surfaces to park cars on. Other people are paving the areas that were lawn so the surface through which water can drain is much smaller. Unless drains are included these areas are more likely to flood in heavy rain, as the water does not have as much ground through which it can soak.

Shelters

Humans make dwellings, which contain different areas for different functions such as sleeping, eating and cooking. They make objects to help them in these actions, tools and furniture such as beds, chairs and tables as well as cloth for warmth and clothes.

Paths and roads

Humans make paths and roads stretching from place to place. Where land has been settled on, humans have changed the landscape. Britain, for example, was once densely wooded but there is little forest left now as over the centuries the trees were felled to provide material for building dwellings, carts, coaches and ships and to provide fuel. Land was also cleared for agriculture.

Agriculture changed the land

When fields emerged they were separated by hedges – hedgerows often signify boundaries that were established centuries ago. Some fields are used for growing crops such as wheat or potatoes whereas other fields are used to graze livestock, particularly sheep and cattle. Up until the twentieth century, horses were the main power source of transport as well as used in farming to pull ploughs and wagons.

Modern transport

Today there are many kinds of vehicles for transport of people and goods. There are land vehicles such as cars, vans and lorries, even sledges in snowbound countries. Railways are another form of land transport, whose arrival saw the demise of inland water traffic on canals and rivers. Today there are underground railways as well as overground ones in many cities. There are water vehicles such as canal barges and container ships for sea transport of goods, and also air vehicles such as aeroplanes that carry people to other countries far more quickly than other forms of transportation.

Aeroplanes also carry foods as cargo, so in the United Kingdom, for example, people can choose to buy strawberries and other fruits or flowers such as roses all year round instead of only having access to them when they are in season.

Street furniture

Streets have street furniture such as signs, seats, postboxes and lampposts. There are different types of buildings, and in buildings there are different shapes used in construction such as circles, squares, triangles, rectangles, columns and flat pieces. Some preschool children are intrigued by the two-dimensional representation of the world and walk round an area with a map checking it against reality.

Talking and doing

The built environment is both inside and outside. Start with the very familiar for the children and talk about what is in these familiar places inside home and school. Then talk about the outside. Children may notice many things but not always have the appropriate or indeed any words for some of the things they see. The rationale of these activities is to focus on the constructed world in which we live, help the children understand the items that make up our world and how these interact with the natural world we have altered.

Our built room

Look around the room where you are. What is in it? What are these things for? What are the names of these things? Are there different kinds of furniture that do the same job? Is something for sitting on always a chair? What else can you sit on? Stools, cushions, arm chairs, hard desk chairs, folding chairs, high chairs, wheel chairs, plastic chairs, fabric chairs, swing chairs, sofas, lavatory seats, bus seats and train seats are some examples.

Furniture

Find pictures in catalogues, magazines or on the Internet of rooms and furniture items. Cut out items, name them and ask the children for what the items are used. Look at different rooms such as kitchens, living rooms, bedrooms and bathrooms.

Buildings all around

What are the jobs of the buildings around you? For what are the buildings used?

Are all shops the same?

Can the children remember different kinds of shops, such a Post Office, supermarket, green grocer, dress shop, shoe shop, bank, department store, pharmacy, petrol station, paper shop and toy shop? What about other buildings, such as a clinic, court, bus station, rail station, police station or hospital?

Different materials

From what materials are local buildings made? Are they made of stone, brick, glass, wood or plastic sheets?

Street shapes

What shapes are there? Look at windows. How many different shapes can the children see? What about doors? Roofs? Look at street furniture; what are their shapes? What shapes are covering the ground in pavements? Paving slabs, cobbles? Make cardboard shapes for paving stones and other coverings and lay out your own pavement on the floor.

Traffic

What kinds of vehicles pass the setting? Some examples to discuss could be buses, cars, vans, lorries, refuse carts, ambulances, police cars, security vans, post vans, taxis, bicycles and motorbikes. What do the children tell you? Are these responses guesses? Why do they say these vehicles?

Find pictures of the different sorts of vehicles and make sets of those that carry people, those that carry goods and other kinds. There are people carriers that are private and those that are there for a job such as police cars, ambulances and taxis.

What kinds of vehicles are on pavements? Push chairs, prams, and wheelie shoppers perhaps?

Ground colour

What colour is the ground? What colour is the road? The pavement? What sort of surface is the road? Is it rough or smooth? What surface has the pavement? What other things are there on the ground (e.g. manhole covers)? Are there different colours on the road surface such as red for a bus lane or blue for a cycle lane? Anything else?

What street furniture is there?

Are there traffic lights? What do they do? Are they on poles or overhead? What effect do they have on the traffic? How do they signal to traffic?

What other objects are there? What colour are these items? Are they all the same size? Which things are big? Which are small? Which is the tallest? The smallest? The widest?

Street signs

What are the signs that can be seen? What shape are they? What are the symbols on them (e.g. mother and child silhouette)? How many different symbols do the children know? What do they mean?

Are there telephone boxes? What are they for? What colour are they? What shape are they? What shapes have they in them? Are the telegraph wires strung from poles?

Shelters and bins

Are there any bus shelters? Seats? Bicycle racks? Postboxes? Are there any litterbins? Is there rubbish anywhere else? Are there recycling bins? What kind? What are the jobs of these different bins?

Writing on the road

Are there markings on the roads, for instance a cycle track marking, yellow lines or white zig zags at the edge of the road? There are stripes across the road at crossings.

Is there any writing on the road? What is it for? What colour is it?

Other streets

What street furniture do the children remember seeing near their home?

Make models of items and design a street.

Playground furniture

What furniture is there in the outside playground? Are there seats? Climbing frames? Swings? Netball posts? Goal posts?

What are the objects the children notice? What are they for?

Are there any marks and drawings on the playground? If so, what are they like? What is their purpose?

Plants in streets

What green things can you see that are plants? Are there algae or mosses on stones or on roofs that can be seen?

Are there any plants growing between cracks in the paving stones or at the bottom of walls? Are plants pushing up through the tarmac, making it bulge up and break to let the stems of a plant through?

Planned plants

Are there any trees or plants with flowers? Do any houses have window boxes?

Compose a photo journal of plants in the street.

Setting plants

What planned plants are there around the setting? Why are they there?

Animals in the street

Ask the children to watch and listen. What animal noises can they hear?

What animals can they see? Why are they in the street?

Hedges and fences

What kinds of hedges and fences can you see? Are they made from growing plants, parts of plants like wood panelling or rails, or man-made substances such as iron and concrete? What is their job?

Green spaces

Are there any green areas around the setting? What and where are they, and why are they there?

Maps

Walk around the setting and ask the children what features they see and what would be important to have on a map so that strangers would know where they were going.

Map walks

Walk around the outdoor area. Ask the children what important things there are to tell new people about. Work out symbol pictures for them.

All together, decide what simple pictures could act as symbols for main items such as the reading corner, computers, coat pegs or whiteboard.

Bird's eye views

Draw a bird's eye view of the room and put the pictures on at the appropriate positions.

Draw a bird's eye view of the outdoor area. This could be drawn on a large piece of construction paper. Sometimes you can obtain an aerial photograph of the area, from Google Earth for example. Have simpler small versions for children to hold.

Cut outs

Some magazines and brochures have photographs of towns and roads. Cut out some pictures, look at them with the children and say the names of things you can see.

12.1 Maps are simplified bird's eye views of where you are. This boy is finding where he is in London Zoo.

Photo journal

If you have a digital camera or similar, ask groups of children to decide what things they would like to take pictures of in the built environment in which they live. First of all the room, then setting, then the grounds and perhaps the town; they could suggest what you could take.

Our street

Do children remember what kinds of things there are on the street? What are these things for? Is there a bridge, a special road sign or a particular building such as a church on the street on which you are located? Is there a special road crossing? If so, how is it marked so people know it is there?

You could look out of the window at the street outside, if that is possible in the location where you are, choose street items to talk about, photograph them and make an 'Our Street' collage using the photographs

---

Outcomes

Through being involved in some of these activities focused on the immediate built environment around where the children live, they may become more observant of their surroundings as they learn the names and purposes of the items in our streets. They will learn the relevant vocabulary but the children should also improve their observational skills by looking at items to seek their purpose. Science begins with observation, then questions. Studying the local built environment is an excellent way of developing such skills.

13

Outside – the natural environment: soils, sky, weather

Summary

The everyday outside world is part of children's own actual experiences. They notice the sky, the weather and hear adults discussing the weather, which affects what they do and what they wear. They notice the ground and its different coverings, stones, soils and vegetation, as well as living things, wild plants and animals. The different kinds of weather have particular names. Wind and rain are particularly noticeable, ranging from light drizzly rain to storms, hurricanes and typhoons. The sky is blue when not full of cloud but sometimes has other colours, such as red, at certain times. Winds are air currents. The top covering of the earth is ice, water or soil. Soils are formed from the wearing down of a variety of rocks, which have been made many years ago in geological time. Different soils have different characteristics depending on the kind of rocks from which they were formed. Certain plants will only grow in particular soils and some animals will only live in certain places, called habitats, with different coverings such as deserts of sand or ice. Organisms exist in these coverings. In soil, some of them help break up the soil and create air pockets, which help with water drainage. Conversely, vegetation on soils helps stop soil being washed away.

Key words

Weather, saturation, spectrum, wavelengths, light, Bernoulli effect, indicator species, soil, particles, fossils, ammonite, carboniferous, coal, sedimentary, igneous, metamorphosis, slate, marble, limestone, sandstone, clouds, cirrus, condensation, crystals, thunderstorms, solar, Beaufort scale, wind speed, thunder, lightning, tornadoes, hurricanes, corona, hot air balloons, weathering, boats, kits, cumulonimbus.

Big ideas

Sky colour

The sky appears blue to us and light appears white. However, light is really a mixture of many colours, the colours of the spectrum. Some of the light is of short wavelength and some of longer length. The combination of colours that make up light are familiar to us as the colours of the rainbow. In a rainbow the light is split into the different wavelengths by water droplets. Longer wavelengths of light, the red, yellow and orange, pass straight through air but much of the shorter wavelengths of light, the violet, blue and green, are absorbed by gas molecules in the air and then spread out through the sky in different directions. Thus the blue sky we see overhead is our seeing some of this scattered blue light. Since you see the blue light from everywhere overhead, the sky looks blue.

Clouds

Clouds are part of the weather, as is seeing the sun when not obscured by clouds. Clouds are not fluffy entities but a collection of water droplets or frozen water (ice crystals) above the earth. When the air above the earth's surface becomes too full of water (saturated) the clouds lose their water and it rains. Technically this action is called precipitation. Clouds have characteristics, different shapes, dimensions and colour. Large thunderclouds are called cumulus, layers of cloud are called stratus and wisps of cloud are called cirrus. Storm clouds are grey to black in colour but cirrus clouds appear wispy white. Clouds form when upward currents of air cool to the temperature at which air becomes saturated (known as the dew point). The water in the air condenses on particles, as shown when you breathe onto a cold surface or breathe out in cold weather and can see the air you expel condense into water droplets. When this phenomenon happens outside at ground level fog occurs, particular in the autumn in England. The colour of clouds depends on the amount of light they reflect from the many particles of water in them.

Winds and air

Wind is part of the everyday world. It is the flow of air that is a mixture of gases, including oxygen, which animals breathe in, and carbon dioxide, which animals breathe out. Green plants take carbon dioxide from the air in the process of photosynthesis and excrete oxygen as a by-product. They excrete carbon dioxide too in their respiratory process.

An air current flows more easily over the top of a flat surface and will lift up the ends of a piece of paper. The air flows faster over the top than the underneath and this causes the piece of paper to rise. This phenomenon is called lift. It is the basis of flight. If a round object, such as a ping pong ball, is in an air current the air moves faster as it goes round the ball. This is because the air has to travel further because of the curve of the ball (or aircraft wing). This is called Bernoulli's theory. A number of exhibits in science centres illustrate this.

Space and solar wind

In outer space there is solar wind caused by the flow of particles from the hot luminous circle called the corona, which surrounds the sun. Researchers are trying to find ways of predicting the solar weather and in particular the aurora, which appears from time to time in the northern hemisphere and is caused by solar wind and particles in it being attracted by the earth's magnetic force. These are the northern lights, or southern lights in the southern hemisphere.

Using winds and measuring them

Winds are rated according to their strength and are measured on a scale. The original was the Beaufort scale, which ranked winds between 53 km/hr and 102 km/hr as gale force winds. Weather forecasters often report the state of the wind, particularly in shipping forecasts. Cyclones and hurricanes are caused by different, severe air movements. Tornadoes are strong rotating columns of air that act like a very strong wind on anything in their paths. A tornado, often called a twister, is in contact with both the ground and the bottom of a cloud. Such clouds are most often of the cumulonimbus kind. Tornadoes are measured on a different scale to normal winds. Humans have always used wind as a source of energy. This is the energy that windmills use to drive their mechanical components, to generate electricity particularly in wind farms and to propel sailing boats. Ships and aircrafts with no engines, such as gliders, rely on the air current for their movement, as do hot air balloons. The wind also plays a part in transporting seeds of some plants away from the parent plant. Birds use rising columns of air, often near to sheer cliffs, to soar upwards.

Wind erosion

Winds wear down rocks (and stone buildings) on the surface of the earth. When winds carry sand, which they pick up from deserts, they act like sand blasters on rock and other things they blow against. When they wear these structures down it is called wind erosion. Winds blow sand and snow into piles called drifts. Water also erodes, as do ice flows. Such erosions played a central part in forming the landscape we see today by scouring out valleys where water and glaciers flowed and breaking down rocks to sediment.

Sky colours

You may have heard the old English saying of 'Red sky at night, shepherd's delight; red sky in the morning, shepherds warning'. Red sky at night usually means good weather the next day. The weather moves from west to east as the earth rotates and changes position. Thus, some parts move away from the sun as other parts move towards it. Red clouds happen when the sun shines on the underside of clouds either in the morning at sunrise or in the evening as the sun sinks in the west at sunset. At this time when the sun is low in the horizon (because the earth is turning so it seems to us it is moving away from the sun) its light passes at a very low angle through the atmosphere. The shorter wavelengths of light in the visible spectrum are scattered; these colours are the greens, blues and violets. Thus, the light that we see is at the red end of the spectrum. In the evening the light illuminates the nearside of rain-bearing clouds, which are moving eastwards. Red skies to the east in a morning are because the weather is traveling east but the rising sun lights up the underside of clouds. These clouds are denser because they are rain clouds carrying water.

Dark skies occur if clouds are very dense, full of crystals or water, or are high in the sky so less light can pass through. When there are lots of clouds they block light and the sky appears dark. Thunderstorms are associated with high cumulonimbus clouds and usually there is a wind accompanying them along with very heavy rain, sometimes ice crystals falling as hail, and lightning. Thunderstorms happen most often towards the end of a hot day.

Rocks

There are three main groups of rocks: igneous, sedimentary and metamorphic. Igneous rocks are formed when molten lava from volcanoes cools. Most of the surface of the earth is covered by igneous rock. Granite is an example, often seen in kitchen tops and buildings. Above this layer is a layer of sedimentary rock. Then there is soil, which differs. It can be like garden soil or sand. Seventy per cent of rocks on the earth are sedimentary ones such as sandstone or limestone, made from sediment that formed from many very small particles of rock that have been pressed together. This has usually happened under water. Limestone often contains the remains of plants and animals that lived on land and were covered by floodwater or in the sea, which appear as fossils. Jet is a hard rock formed from pressure on plant stems. Coal is the remains of plants that lived in the carboniferous period and were preserved in water, then becoming covered with sediments and hardened to coal rock.

Kinds of rock

Rocks such as limestone, gravels, sand, silt and clay are formed from sediments of various rocks. Lava stones or pumices are formed when hot volcanic lava from a volcano meets water. Pumices have lots of air pockets. Metamorphic rocks have been changed from igneous to sedimentary, usually by intense pressure or temperatures. Everyday examples you may see are slate as roof tiles, clay as bricks, granite worktops and marble.

Soils

Soil is made up of small bits of broken rock called stones that have been made by a number of processes that include wind and water erosion, frost action, chemical activity and action of plants. So it is a mix of the minerals from the rock and biological material such as dead leaves from plants and the remains of animals. The soil particles are separated by air pockets. Some soils have few spaces, such as clay, while others such as sandy soils have many and water runs through them easily. Plants are important ground cover and cut down erosion by covering the soil and binding it. When vegetation is removed soil erosion occurs as topsoil is washed or blown away.

Soil and plants and animals

Living things affect the formation of soil. Some animals mix soils when they make their burrows, especially earthworm burrows. The roots of plants make channels in the soil too as they grow through it. The type of soil affects which kinds of plants grow. Heathers and silver birch trees, for example, thrive on acid soils whereas rose bushes do well on clay soils. The environment also influences what animals and plants live there. Some animals prefer dark, moist conditions. Animals such as woodlice live under leaves and stones where it is damp and humid. Mosses also need to live in moist conditions because their sex cells need water to swim to another plant for fertilization.

Talking and doing

People talk about the weather a lot; they notice whether the sky contains clouds or if the sun is visible, and so it is a topic that the children hear much about. They notice the sun in the sky and how shadows are formed. They experience the feel of the sun and of air on them. The kind of weather affects them in terms of what they wear and what they can do. Similarly, night and day are very much a part of children's lives. They tend to go to bed when it is night and get up for the daytime. Children see rocks as stones and pebbles on the ground, in soil and as parts of buildings and other human artefacts. They may even have seen fossils in rocks. The activities suggested in this chapter provide experience of natural phenomena. These experiences will provide a sound basis for later education about them.

The sun

Ask about the sun. When do the children see the sun? When the world is dark can they see the sun? When it is night-time, what can they see in the sky? Is there any light generated by what they can see?

No sun

How do we see things when there is no sunlight? What can stop the sunlight from reaching us?

The feel of the sun

What does the sun feel like on your hand?

Choose several items such as a piece of paper or a piece of cloth, e.g. a towel or t-shirt. Feel them, say what they feel like. Are they hot, cold? Leave them somewhere in the sun for 30 minutes and then feel them again. Leave them longer, measure the time. What do the items feel like then? Do they all feel the same? What is different? How do they compare to how these they felt before they were put in the sun?

You can use a lamp to represent the sun when there is no sun.

Night and day

Look in picture storybooks and ask children to identify night and day in the pictures. Talk about what is night. Ask about the differences between night and day.

What does day mean to the children? What does night mean?

How long does night last? Is it always the same length in our country? What happens?

Sun, moon and stars

Where is the sun at night? Where is the moon in the day? Where are the stars in the day? Can you ever see the moon during the day? Is the moon always the same size? Can you always see the stars and the moon at night? Can you see the sun every day?

What is in the sky?

What else is in the sky? What human-made things can we see in the sky? What animals can we see in the sky?

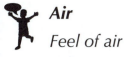

Air

Feel of air

What happens if a child blows air on the top of his or her hand? What does it feel like? Can s/he blow softly? More strongly? What is the difference?

What happens if they blow through a straw? Does the wind they make them feel the same as when they blow without using the straw?

Design and make an air blower

What can be used to blow air instead of a straw? Try rolling up pieces of different paper to make tubes. Which paper makes the best blow tube?

Air bubbles

Blow air through a straw in water. What happens? Where have the bubbles come from?

Unscrew the top of a fizzy drink bottle; what happens? Pour out some fizzy drink into a small cup; what happens as the liquid fills the cup if it is poured quickly? The bubbles in fizzy drinks are from gas dissolved in the liquid under pressure. As soon as the pressure is released the gas comes out of the solution, creating bubbles.

Breathing out water

What do children feel if they breathe out on the back of their hand?

Put a plate or mirror in the fridge if you can; take it out after a while and ask a child what temperature the surface of the plate feels like and what it looks like. Then ask them to breathe out onto the surface; what do they see? The water droplets are from the water in the air in their breath that has condensed. When you breathe out in cold weather you see white in front of you like a cloud, which is the air in your breath.

Air lift

Can blowing on a floppy piece of paper make it lift up?

Show the children the way that air can lift things by asking then to hold a flat piece of paper (half of a sheet of computer paper for example) just below their mouth. Notice what the paper does. Is it sticking out in front of the child's mouth? Then ask them to blow across the top of the paper; this is air moving faster than the air underneath the paper. What happens?

Make wind

What happens when you wave your arms about near a few pieces of light paper, e.g. tissue paper, on a desk? You have made an air current! Read the story of the three little pigs and the 'big bad' wolf (if it is not culturally inappropriate) and how he huffed and puffed and blew the house down.

Drying things

Wind can dry things too by helping water to evaporate.

Do people where you live put washing out when it is wet? What happens to the washing after it has been outside? What helps the washing lose its water and dry out? Do you see people put washing out to dry when it is raining? Why not?

Fans

When it is hot some people use fans to move the air past them to cool them a bit. The air current can increase evaporation from their skin and warmth is taken out of them into the air, thus cooling them.

Fan search

Find out different kinds of fans.

Make a fan

What sorts of things would children use to make such a fan? What are their ideas? Folding card into zig zags is one way; cutting out a circle and fixing it to a lollipop stick or other straight but stiff item (rulers are useful to for this) is another.

Fan inquiry – flapping a fan

How many flaps of their fan are needed to move a piece of tissue 1 cm by 1 cm, 4 cm by 4 cm, 6 cm by 6 cm, etc? Is there a difference in the number of flaps needed? Can the children explain what they notice?

Clouds

What are the clouds today?

Ask the question each day at the same time. Are there clouds in different shapes? Is the sky all grey with a sheet of cloud? Are there fluffy clouds with a blue sky or no clouds at all?

Cloud colour

What colour are the clouds? Keep a chart to fill in on a wall, in a journal or on a computer. Talk about what colour the clouds were last week – were they the same as this week? Were they different?

Are clouds always the same?

Were different kinds of clouds associated with certain weather? What are rain clouds like? What are clouds like on a warm day?

Weather chart:

Day	Time	Kind of weather	Clouds seen 1: shape and colour	Clouds seen 2: shape and colour	Clouds seen 3: shape and colour

If you look in the morning, and then again at home time, are the clouds still there? If so, are they still the same kind?

You may be able to find photographs of clouds on the Internet or in magazines and newspapers, similar to those the children see; fix them to a paper chart or import into an electronic one.

Cloud photo journal and diary

Every day for a week, using the digital camera, let a child be a cloud photographer and take a picture of the sky to make a cloud gallery. Each child could upload the photographs they took to their portfolio, if they have one.

Look and talk about cloud shape, colour and number of clouds over the weeks.

Clothes for weather

Talk about the different types of weather. What do they feel like? What kind of clothes do you wear for the different kinds of weather in your country?

In what weather would you wear the following clothes: wellington boots, souwester, sun hat, sandals, shorts, pullover, trainers, scarf, gloves, raincoat, shoes, waterproof, t-shirt, thick socks, boots.

When do people use an umbrella? What about a parasol, sunshade or a fan? What do people use these things for?

Have the children draw pictures of clothes associated with the following:

- dry weather
- cold weather
- warm weather
- hot weather
- wet weather
- drizzle
- light rain
- heavy rain
- snowy
- icy.

Can you measure how much rain falls in a day?

How could the children find out how much rain falls on the playground during a day? What do they think? How can you measure the rain if it is collected in a container? What sort of container is best to use? One you can see through, such as a plastic beaker or a plastic drinks bottle with the top cut off, or a coloured plastic jug you cannot see through? Why did the children choose one over the other?

Sun path

How can you tell if the sun moves across the sky?

If you have a window through which the sun can be seen, you could instruct the children put a sticky paper cut-out or blob of yellow modelling clay over the sun as seen from a particular spot in the classroom (make sure the children do not look directly at the sun; this can damage their eyes). Do this every hour and see what happens.

Sundial

Put a stick in a tray of sand or fix the stick in a lump of modelling clay in a tray when the sun is shining outside so there is a shadow on the sand or tray. Lay a strip of paper or string along the shadow that the stick makes on the sand. Put a flag above this mark to remind you which was the first shape of the shadow watching. Look again each hour and mark the line of the shadow of the stick on the sand; what do the children notice? Can the children explain why the shadow has moved?

Shadows

If a child puts something in front of a beam of light when standing before a plain wall they make a shadow. Ask them to try it, using a part of their body such as a hand or foot.

Can a child use their hand to make a shape like a rabbit with ears? What other shape can they make?

Shadow puppets

You can design and cut out different shapes, and if you fix them to a stick you have stick silhouette puppets. Then children can make up and tell a story to others. If the children hold up the silhouettes on sticks in front of a screen and behind a strong light source the shapes will appear on the screen to an audience on the other side. You can do this with capital letter shapes or numerals and have the children say what letter is being shown. The nearer the shape is to the light source the bigger the shadow is. The nearer you are to the light source, the greater the magnifying effect. The Gruffalo's child's shadow would not have been as big as it was in the story as the moon was so very far away.

Rainbow

Tell the children the colours of the rainbow (Richard Of York Gave Battle In Vain – red, orange, yellow, green, blue, indigo, violet – is a useful mnemonic to remember them and their order). Have them colour in a rainbow using the appropriate colours, so they learn the wavelengths of light and their order.

Puddle rainbows

Look at oil in puddles or on the bubbles blown from bubble mixture; often you can see the colours of the rainbow on their surfaces.

Evidence of weathering

Are there any buildings or rocks nearby that have been smoothed? Some of the gargoyles that stick out at the edge of church roofs have had their features blunted by the effect of weather over the centuries.

Wind erosion

You can show children the effect of wind erosion by having a pile of sand in two plastic aquaria, three-quarters of the way along the base of each tank.

This is a precaution so that you do not blow the sand out of the tank into their eyes. The children could wear goggles like practical scientists instead.

Point the jet of a balloon pump at the pile and see what happens. Does the wind jet affect the sand pile? What happens to the pile? What happens if the jet is pointed at flat sand?

Rain erosion

In two plastic seed trays or again using the plastic aquaria, take some earth and pile it at one end to make slopes, so you have two trays each with a slope of soil at one end.

Into one slope place lots of sticks (tooth picks or small twigs) to represent trees. You could make a slope with pieces of earth covered with grass if they are available. Leave the other slope bare.

Have a small watering can. Measure the amount of water you put in to get the children used to measuring. Water the slope with 'trees'. Water the slope without the trees. What happens? If you have grass, what happens to that slope?

This is a very simple demonstration of the washing away of soil by water.

Measure a puddle

On a windy day, talk about the weather. Is it windy? Is it sunny? Pour some water onto a patch outside where you know that a puddle forms in a light dip in the ground when it rains. Measure the circumference of the puddle – draw a line with chalk if the puddle is on concrete, otherwise place some small sticks (with flags if you like, the children can make them) stuck into a small amount of modelling clay around the edge of the water to mark the level.

Look again at lunch time – what has happened? With another set of flags (these could be a different colour) or chalk draw around the edge of the puddle. Look again later, and before home time. Take another look the next day if it is possible to leave the markers out. The disappearance of water could be due to action of wind. It could be due to the water draining away or from the heat of the sun causing water to evaporate. The disappearance of the water could be a mixture of all three but the activity is a useful one to show that puddles do eventually disappear.

Doing things with wind – boats and rafts

Ask the children what you need to make a raft or a boat with a sail. You will need a water tank, sink or a large bowl to be the pond.

Make a small raft with polystyrene trays, pieces of flat polystyrene packaging or flat plastic vegetable trays. You can attach a sail by inserting a stick (or pencil) into the polystyrenes. For the other trays you will have to fit the mast with a blob of modelling clay. What do boats need in order to move across still water – engines are not allowed, nor are rowers! If the children say wind, then let them try. How will they make the wind? What happens?

Blowing a raft or boat

How can it be made to go faster? Perhaps someone will suggest a sail. Attach sails to the mast. A piece of paper can have holes pierced in it to allow the mast through although a piece of sticky tap at the top of the mast will stop the sail descending. Cloth can be used, the lighter the better. How can the children measure the speed at which the boats move? Can they use a second timer? Is thick paper or card more effective than thin paper? Can the children investigate and find out the answer? Have a boat race!

Blow, blow!

Where do the children need to blow to make the boat move faster with child wind power? What other wind sources could be used?

Floating in the air

Blow up some balloons. Attach a long string to the neck of the balloon where it is tied off to prevent the air from escaping. Also, attach a string to the neck of an uninflated balloon. Go outside when it is windy. What do the children think will happen to the two balloons, blown up and non-blown up? What make them think that? What are their reasons? Let the balloons go but hold onto the string. What happens? Why? What is the difference between the blown up balloon and the non-blown up one? Air is light, and when contained, will blow away.

Kites

What other things will be taken up by wind? What do the children suggest? You could attach pieces of tissue paper to pieces of heavier paper – perhaps as long strips – and take them outside. Perhaps the children would like to cut out birds or other shapes, attach them to a string or pieces of thread, take them outside and throw them into the wind?

Ask the children, 'Have you seen a kite? Could you fly a kite? Could you make a kite?' Try using straws covered with tissue paper and a piece of thread attached for the children to hold. Ask, 'What happens if you just let your kite go? Do you have to throw your kite into the wind stream to pull the kite behind you? Will the kite float if there is no wind?'

Soils – different kinds

Have containers (such as plastic vegetable containers from the supermarket) and use a trowel to obtain different kinds of soil for the children to look at. Try some sand from the sand tray, some compost or peat, some garden soil, some clay soil or even art clay and some gravel. If you have garden soil obtain some of that too.

Ask the child to say what is inside each container. What does it looks like? What colour is it?

Air in soil

With some garden soil ask children what happens if you place a small amount into water. Do so and watch. Usually some air bubbles come out because air is trapped between solid particles.

Wet and dry

Look at a pile of dry soil and a pile of wet soil. What is the difference between the two? Are they the same colour? Do they look the same? What difference has adding water to the dry soil made?

Draining soils

What happens if you put water onto each different soil? What do the children think? Why do they think that? If you can, use plastic drinks bottles with the top cut off and inverted to make a funnel, then place some kitchen towel or jeye cloth across the hole so that the soil bits will not go through. Put the same amount (large scoop or small beaker-full) into the funnels and place each into the top of the lower half of the bottle. Arrange the bottles in a row and make sure everyone knows what sort of soil is in each funnel. Sand, garden soil, compost and gravel can be easily obtained, plus clay soil if you can get it.

Fair test

How can you make this a fair test to see which soil lets water through the most quickly? Have children with the same amount of water at each soil station. Position another child to watch the water go through and say 'Done!' when there is no more in the funnel to pass through.

Which soil lets the water through the fastest? Ask for someone to say 'Go', to signal that the children should start pouring their water into the funnel.

Sorting rocks

What different kinds of stones are around you?

Perhaps there are stones used in buildings or pavements?

Rock hunt

What hard surfaces that could be rock are in the setting?

Try to find some rock pieces such as granite, pumice (volcanic ash), limestone, marble chips, chalk, flint, slate, gravel and sand. Ask the children what these rock pieces are like.

Rock in buildings

Where have they seen rock in buildings or at home? Many kitchens have granite work-tops these days and churches have marble floors.

Fossils

Have the children ever seen a fossil? Pieces of limestone in some buildings or walls often have shapes in them from animals that became fossilized, particularly a kind called ammonites, which look like curled, flat snail.

What's under a stone?

Some living things make their homes under stones.

Ask the children what they think it is like under a stone. Is it dark, damp, cold?

Have a look under a stone, brick or even a bucket after it has been outside for a few days. What do the children think they might find? Are there any live plants under the stones? Are there any dead parts of plants? How can you tell if what you find is a plant and alive?

13.1 What is under stones? This girl is finding out by looking; an important part of learning science is observing.

Woodlice, slugs, earthworms (if there is soil) and sometimes centipedes are the likely animals, along with dead leaves. They love to live in damp places.

Plants under stones

Look at a patch of grass. What colour is it? Place a stone, brick or bucket on a patch of grass plants. Leave it for a few days. What do the children think they will they see you then pick up the cover? Will the grass plants look the same? Why do they think this? Lift the cover; what do they see?

Plants need soil

Pull up a weed (a plant growing where humans do not want it!). Groundsel plants are ideal, and Shepherds' Purse is an excellent specimen for this activity. Otherwise a grass plant will suffice.

Lay the plant on a piece of white paper. Ask the children which parts they usually see and which parts they do not. What are these parts called? What do they do? Why can the children see all the parts of the plant now?

Seeds and soil

Look at a packet of seeds. Ask the children what we do with seeds. What do we put them in? Why do seeds need planting? What can you plant them in?

If they say soil, ask them what sort of soil.

Growing seeds

Obtain small plastic plant pots, yoghurt pots or polystyrene coffee cups and make sure the non-plant pots have a hole for drainage. Add different kinds of soils. Put different kinds of soil in each pot, then add a few seeds and cover them with the same type of soil. Use sand, garden soil, compost and gravel in different plant pots. Stand them all in a tray. Ask the children what else the seeds need besides something to grow in. They will probably say that seeds need water to grow. If so, ask them how much water, and should each seed have the same amount or a different amount of water? To be fair use the same amount of water for each pot. Watch what happens. The seeds will develop in the appropriate growing medium with some water in the dark if some children suggest light. The seedlings need light once their shoot emerges so they can photosynthesize. Without light their leaves and shoots will not become green (like grass that has had light cut off from it).

Thirsty seeds

Leave some seeds in a see-though plastic beaker with nothing but a small amount of water (the same amount as the seeds in the plant pots were given so it is fair and the only variable is what the seeds are contained in) and see what happens. Leave some seeds out in a beaker and do not give them water.

What do the children think will happen? Why?

What does happen? Look every day and make a seed report. Photograph the seeds daily to make a photo diary of growing seeds.

Outcomes

Through being actively involved in explorations of their everyday surroundings, not just limited to the learning setting, the children should begin to develop an awareness and basic understanding of the natural environment around them. They should also gain awareness of the effect humans and other things, such as the weather, can have on the environment.

References and further reading

Alderson, P. (2000) *Young Children's Rights: Beliefs and Practices*. London: Jessica Kingsley.

Alexander, R. (2008) *Towards Dialogic Teaching: Rethinking Classroom Talk*. Cambridge: Dialogs.

Allen, G. (2011) *Early Intervention: The Next Steps. An Independent Report to Her Majesty's Government*. London: HM Government. Online. Available www. dwp.gov.uk/docs/early-intervention-next-steps.pdf

ASE (2010) *Be Safe*! 4th edition. Hatfield: Association for Science Education.

Blenkin, G. M. and Kelly, A. V. (1996) *Early Childhood Education: A Developmental Curriculum*. London: Paul Chapman.

Bradley, H. (1996) *Fractured Identities: Changing Patterns of Inequality*. New York: Wiley.

Brenneman, K. and Louro, I. F. (2008) Science Journals in the Preschool Classroom. *Early Childhood Education Journal*, 36: 113–119.

Broadhead, P. (2006) Developing an Understanding of Young Children's Learning Through Play: The Place of Observation, Interaction and Reflection. *British Educational Research Journal*, 32(2): 191–207.

Bruner, J. (1990) *Acts of Meaning*. Cambridge, MA: Harvard University Press.

Chin, C. (2007) Questioning in Science Classrooms: Approaches that Stimulate Productive Thinking. *Journal of Research in Science Teaching*, 44(6): 815–843.

CLEAPSS (2010) *Guidance Leaflets*. Online. Available www.cleapss.org.uk/primary/primary-resources/primary-guidance-leaflets

DfCFS (2004) *United Nations Conventions on the Rights of the Child: Priorities for Action*. Online. Available www.education.gov.uk/publications/eOrderingDownload/01099-2009BKT-EN.pdf

DfEs (2006) *Ethnicity and Education: The Evidence on Minority Ethnic Pupils Aged 5–16*. Online. Available www.education.gov.uk/rsgateway/DB/RRP/u014955/index.shtml

DfEs (2011) *Supporting Families in the Foundation Years*. Available http://media.education.gov.uk/assets/files/pdf/s/supporting%20families%20in%20the%20foundation%20 years.pdf

Eshach, H. and Fried, M. N. (2005) Should Science be Taught in Early Childhood? *Journal of Science Education and Technology, 14*(3): 315–336.

Gopnik, A. (2009) *The Philosophical Baby: What Children's Minds Tell Us About Truth, Love, and the Meaning of Life*. New York: Farrar, Straus and Giroux.

Gopnik, A. and Seiver, E. (2009) Reading Minds. *Zero to Three, 30*(2): 28–32.

Halliday, M. A. K. (1993) Towards a Language-based Theory of Education. *Linguistics in Education, 5*: 93–116.

Harlen, W. (Ed) (2010) *Principles and Big Ideas of Science Education*. Hatfield: Association for Science Education.

Katz, P. (2011) A Case Study of the Use of Internet Photobook Technology to Enhance Early Childhood 'Scientist' Identity. *Journal of Science Education and Technology, 20*(5): 525–536.

Katz, P. (2012) Using Photo Books to Encourage Young Children's Science Identities. *Journal of Emergent Science, 3*.

Lancaster, Y. P. and Broadbent, V. (2003) *Listening to Young Children*. Maidenhead: Open University Press.

Lind, K. K. (1999) Science in Early Childhood: Developing and Acquiring Fundamental Concepts and Skills. In *Dialogue on Early Childhood Science, Mathematics and Technology Education*. Washington, DC: American Association for the Advancement of Science.

Lyons, T. and Quinn, F. (2010) *Choosing Science: understanding the declines in senior high school science enrolments*. Research Report to the Australian Science Teachers Association. UNE.

Mercer, N. (2000) *Words and Minds: How We Use Language to Think Together*. London: Routledge.

Mercer, N., Dawes, L., Wegerif, R. and Sams, C. (2004) Reasoning as Scientists: Ways of Helping Children to Use Language to Learn Science. *British Educational Research Journal, 30*(3): 359–377.

Morrison, C. M. and Conway, M. A. (2010) First Words and Memories. *Cognition, 116*(1): 23–32.

Moyles, J. R. (1989) *Just Playing? The Role and Status of Play in Early Childhood Education*. Milton Keynes: Open University Press.

Palmer, I. (2011) *The Understanding of Plants and Animals of 8 Bilingual Pupils Aged 3–4 Attending an English Inner City State Primary School*. Submitted.

Patrick, P. and Tunnicliffe, S. D. (2011) What Plants and Animals Do Early Childhood and Primary Students Name? Where Do They See Them? *Journal of Science Education and Technology, 20*(5): 630–642.

Piaget, J. and Inhelder, B. (2000) *The Psychology of Childhood*. (H. Weaver, Trans.) New York: Basic Books.

Pines, A. L. and West, L. H. T. (1986) Conceptual Understanding and Science Learning: An Interpretation of Research Within a Sources-of-Knowledge Framework. *Science Education, 70*(5): 583–604.

Purple Mash (2010) *Purple Mash Educational Resource*. Online. Available www.purplemash.com

Rogoff, B. (1990) *Apprenticeship in Thinking: Cognitive Development in Social Context*. New York: Oxford University Press.

Sackes, M., Trundle, K. C., Bell, R. L. and O'Connell, A. (2011) The Influence of Early Science Experience in Kindergarten on Children's Immediate and Later Science Achievement: Evidence from the Early Childhood Longitudinal Study. *Journal of Research in Science Teaching, 48*(2): 217–235.

Scribner-MacLean, M. (1996) Science at Home. *Science and Children, 33*: 44–48.

Shepherd, J. (2011) Almost a Quarter of State School Pupils are from an Ethnic Minority. *The Guardian*, 22nd June.

Sheridan, M. (1990). *Spontaneous Play in Early Childhood*. Windsor: NFER-Nelson Publishing Co. Ltd.

Spektor-Levy, O., Baruch, Y. K. and Mevarech, Z. (2011) Science and Scientific Curiosity in Pre-School: The Teacher's Point of View. *International Journal of Science Education*, 1–228. iFirst article.

Tough, J. (1977) *The Development of Meaning*. London: George Allen and Unwin.

Tunnicliffe, S. D. (1989) *Living Things – Think and Do*, Oxford: Basil Blackwell.

Tunnicliffe, S. D. (1990) *Challenge Science – Living Things*, Oxford: Basil Blackwell.

Tunnicliffe, S. D. (2004) Where does the Drink Go? *Primary Science Review, 85*: 8–10.

Tunnicliffe, S. D. and Patrick, P. (2012) *Zoo Talk*. New York: Springer.

Tymms, P. and Harlen, W. (2009) *Perspectives on Education: Primary Science*. London: The Wellcome Trust.

Tytler, R., Osbourne, J., Williams, G., Tytler, K. and Cripps Clarke, J. (2008) *Opening up Pathways: Engagement in Science, Technology, Mathematics and Engineering, (STEM) across the Primary-Secondary School transition. Canberra. Department of Education, Employment and Workplace Relations*. Available http://www.dest.gov.au/NR/ndonrtyres/IBCIZECD-81ED-43DEOF698F8A6F44EZ /23337/Finaljune140708pdfversion.pdf

Vygotsky, L. S. (1962) *Thought and Language*. Cambridge, MA: MIT Press.

Vygotsky, L. S. (1978) *Mind in Society: The Development of Higher Psychological Processes*. Cambridge, MA: Harvard University Press.

Wellington, J. and Osborne, J. F. (2010) *Language and Literacy in Science Education*. Buckingham: Open University.

Wertsch, J. V. (1985) *Vygotsky and the Social Formation of Mind*. Cambridge, MA: Harvard University Press.

2simple (2010) *Simple City*. Online. Available www.2simple.com/simplecity

Index